The Anatomy & Development of the STOCK CAR

Dr. John Craft

Motorbooks International
Publishers & Wholesalers ®

Dedication

For Betty Jo who always knew

First published in 1993 by Motorbooks International Publishers & Wholesalers, PO Box 2, 729 Prospect Avenue, Osceola, WI 54020 USA

Motorbooks International books are also available at discounts in bulk quantity for industrial or sales-promotional use. For details write to Special Sales Manager at the Publisher's address

Library of Congress Cataloging-in-Publication Data

Craft, John.
 The anatomy and development of the stock car/John Craft.
  p. cm.
 Includes index.
 ISBN 0-87938-800-5
 1. Automobiles, Racing—History. I. Title.
 TL236.C69   1993
 629.228'0973—dc20   93-27505

On the front cover: *The current generation of the Chevrolet Lumina wears the paint of Darrell Waltrip's former sponsors as he blurs past a grandstand full of stock car fans.* Dr. John Craft

Printed and bound in the United States of America

Contents

Introduction   4

Chapter 1 **Strictly Stock: NASCAR's First Decade**   6
Smokey Yunick: Testing the Rules   18

Chapter 2 **Redefining 'Stock': The Sixties &
Seventies on the Circuit**   27
Wayne Torrenoo: Veteran of the Tire Wars   80
Ralph Moody: Truly Legendary   82
Dick Hutcherson: A Winner in Many Eras   87

Chapter 3 **Racing into the Future: The Modern
Era, 1972–1994**   91
Mark Davis: Dissecting a Modern NASCAR Stock Car   142
Robert Yates: Successfully Climbing the Ladder   154
Bill Tower: The Inside Story of the Modern Engine   157

Index   160

Introduction

In the beginning, there was 'shine—moonshine, that is: white lightning, mountain dew. And in the late thirties, that incendiary, unstable-around-open-flames brew had a devoted following of thirsty connoisseurs anxious to buy all they could get. Slaking that bibulous demand were dozens of independent "distillers" who worked by the light of the moon in remote mountain "hollers." The obvious problem was, of course, the geographic distance between their rural stills and the dry palates of their urban customers—and the revenuers.

You see, though the production of home-brewed whiskey was—and still is—a respected Appalachian tradition dating back to the earliest days of the thirteen colonies, it was also highly illegal. Not because it was dangerous to your health, you understand. The safety-nazis who might have railed about the unsanitary brewing conditions of most moonshiners and the deleterious effect of their distillate on a body's liver were still decades in the future. And moonshine didn't receive the government's enforcement attention because alcohol, in general, was illegal. Carry Nation's prohibitionist ax had been broken into splinters by popular demand in 1933. Most of the United States had happily resumed its relationship with Demon Rum and John Barleycorn—although dry counties still exist in the rural Southland.

The real problem for enterprising home brewers in the late thirties and forties was taxes—more specifically, the taxes they failed to pay to Uncle Sam and his local cousins, on the countless mason jars of 'shine they sold. Forget about other old saws you might have heard, Hell truly hath no fury like a tax man scorned.

So the government set out to shut down every mountainside still it could locate. But there's the rub: it didn't find all that many. The rugged topography of the Blue Ridge and Great Smoky ranges worked against the revenuer's search-and-destroy missions just as surely as did the moonshiner's nocturnal working habits. And let's not forget the traditional circumspection of many mountain folk. Talking to strangers at length—let alone informing on successful, albeit illegal, local business ventures during the Depression years—just wasn't part of the culture.

So it was that the revenuers began to target the supply lines that linked rural production facilities with urban consumers. You might say that was the moment stock car racing actually got its start, though the first of-

ficial green flag was still years in the future. Once the tax agents started targeting transportation routes, mechanically minded 'shine runners wasted little time making sure their cars stayed one step ahead of the law. The modifications these homespun hot rodders began making to the ordinary American sedan they used to complete their nightly runs were the first steps toward the purpose-built bullets that are currently blistering NASCAR tracks on the Winston Cup circuit.

Big, boxy General Motors (GM), Mopar, and Ford Motor Company (FoMoCo) sedans were the cars of choice for most 'shine runners, owing to their capacity. Stripping out unneeded interior components and replacing them with the gear required to transport several hundred gallons of alcohol turned the cars into stealth moonshine tankers. Of course, the weight penalty incurred by carrying half a ton of moonshine made even the fastest cars of the day easy targets for revenue agents and their unburdened pursuit vehicles. The extra avoirdupois also took a toll on parts. Both were reasons for the mechanical modifications that 'shine runners started making to their cars. Wider wheels that permitted the use of larger-than-stock tires were standard equipment on many cars used for bootlegging. So, too, were heavier hubs, stiffer springs, and two shocks for each wheel. It's no coincidence that many of these same modifications later found their way onto stock car starting grids. In fact, according to racing legend and former 'shine runner Robert ("Junior") Johnson, "A good race car today is nothing but a good 1940s moonshine car, refined."

The extra horsepower needed to keep revenuers in the rearview mirror was generated by both conventional and unconventional means. Boring and stroking to gain cubic inches was commonplace. Altering valve timing and modifying head castings to improve intake and exhaust flow were also standard fare. Sometimes, larger, more-powerful-than-stock engines lifted from other car lines or manufacturers found a new home under the hood of 'shine cars, too. And even such supposedly high-tech, up-to-date horsepower enhancers as McCullough superchargers and aircraft industry turbochargers were sometimes used to put a little extra distance between 'shine drivers and pursuing law enforcement officers.

It took incredible driving skill to master a hulking, high-horsepower moonshine car—especially at triple-digit velocities on winding, poorly paved mountain roads in the dead of the night and running with the lights off, which is how stealthy 'shine runners often chose to operate. Junior Johnson claimed, "To this day, I have never driven a race car that could compare with some of the liquor cars that I drove. I've never driven as fast on a racetrack as I have on the road. Course, when I quit racing, we was only running about 180 down the backstretch [at Daytona]." After negotiating undeveloped rural roads at those speeds in pitch-blackness with federal and local agents in hot pursuit, racing must have seemed like child's play to early stock car drivers, like Johnson, who had spent time running liquid lightning.

Indeed, that's pretty much how stock car racing got its start—as a recreational activity for 'shine drivers during their off-hours. The perhaps instinctive tendency for one man to test the performance of his car (camel, horse, armadillo) against that of another resulted in informal races on county roads and fairground ovals. At first, these competitions were attended only by those involved, but in time, enterprising promoters began to see the possibilities of organizing a revenue-producing sport around 'shine car competitions. The rest, as they say, is history.

Chapter 1

Strictly Stock:
NASCAR's First Decade

The date was December 14, 1947. The place was the old Streamline Hotel in Daytona Beach, Florida, and the man with the plan was William Henry Getty ("Big Bill") France, Sr. The occasion was a meeting of thirty-five racing promoters from all across the United States, and their purpose was to lend some order to the uncoordinated chaos that often characterized the burgeoning sport

At 6 feet (ft) 4in and 240lb, Big Bill France cut an imposing figure. His ideas were larger still, and they led directly to the creation of NASCAR. NASCAR Archives

of stock car racing. France, the chairman of that three-day gathering, presided over the deliberations that would ultimately lead to the birth of the most successful race-sanctioning organization in the country: the National Association for Stock Car Auto Racing (NASCAR).

France and NASCAR's cofounders formally incorporated the new organization two months later, in February of 1948. The express purpose of the association was to "unite all stock car racing under one set of rules and to set up a benevolent fund and a national point standings system whereby only one stock car driver will be crowned national champion." Three different divisions were set up by the sanctioning body: Strictly Stock, Modified Stock, and Roadsters. The Strictly Stock Division was destined to enjoy the greatest success: it would ultimately evolve into the Winston Cup series, which today is the most popular form of racing in the United States.

The rules of the Strictly Stock Division were the essence of simplicity: cars deemed legal for competition were required to remain unmodified in all ways save for the addition of a reinforcement ring in the right front wheel, designed to keep the lug nuts from pulling through. Rim widths had to remain factory stock, and no change in offset or back spacing was permitted. Tires were the weak link, since they, too, had to remain unmodified. Slicks were not permitted, but any other type of treaded, factory-produced tire could be mounted. The trouble was that none of the regular production rubber that was available in the early fifties was up to the rigors of racing. Even the truck tires that many racers opted to use failed with exceeding regularity. At times, so many bits and pieces of blown tires would litter a racetrack that driving over them actually became a hazard in itself. Broken windshields, punctured radiators, and driver injuries all resulted from impacts with the chunks of tire carcass that were tossed up by passing cars. The "debris-on-the-track" yellow caution flags that are sometimes used by NASCAR officials to bunch up racing packs and enliven on-track action today, were a very real necessity during the earliest days of Strictly Stock competition.

Though NASCAR allowed liberal changes away from stock in alignment specifications, it did not allow alteration of the suspension components to which those tires translated surface irregularities. Leaf springs were

Time Line

1947 NASCAR is formed at a meeting in Daytona Beach, Florida.

1949 The first Strictly Stock race is held on a 3/4-mile (mi) dirt track in Charlotte, North Carolina. The Strictly Stock Division will be renamed the Grand National Division within six months of this race. Oldsmobilebegins a horsepower race by fitting its biggest engine in the smallest car in the line.

1950 Darlington International Raceway opens to become the circuit's first super speedway. Ford wins its first Grand National race.

1951 Chrysler introduces the hemi-headed Firepower V-8.

1953 Hudson introduces the 7X dual-carburetor engine at the request of NASCAR drivers. This is one of the first instances of direct factory support for the Grand National circuit. Dodge wins its first Grand National race.

1954 Dodge, Ford, and Mercury receive their first overhead valve V-8 engines. The flathead becomes a dinosaur. Chrysler introduces the first 300hp regular production automobile, the Chrysler 300.

1955 Plymouth, Chevrolet, and Pontiac all receive their first overhead valve V-8s. Chevrolet wins its first Grand National race.

1956 Ford hires Pete De Paolo to organize a factory-backed racing effort.

1957 Ford introduces a supercharged version of the 312-cubic inch (ci) Y-block to counter Chevrolet's new fuel-injected 283ci small-block. President Red Curtice of GM persuades the AMA to ban factory-backed racing programs. Holman and Moody is formed when De Paolo leaves Ford employment. Ford pulls out of racing shortly afterwards.

1958 Goodyear enters NASCAR racing, and a tire war with Firestone begins. Ford and Chevrolet both introduce their first "big-block" engines.

1959 Holman and Moody builds a fleet of 430ci-powered Thunderbirds for sale to anyone with $5,500. Daytona International Speedway opens, and Ralph Moody takes the track's first hot laps in a Holman and Moody T-bird. Plymouth introduces the 361 big-block motor and wins its first Grand National race.

1960 Ford hires the Wood brothers to conduct stock car tests, before returning to the circuit. Full-floating rear hubs become mandatory.

1961 Holman and Moody receives factory backing from Ford following the Daytona 500. Ford Galaxies receive four-speed Borg-Warner transmissions as an option. Ford's big-block grows to 390ci, Plymouth's to 413ci, and Chevrolet's to 409ci. Pontiac offers an "over-the-counter" 421ci big-block.

1962 Chrysler intermediates become completely unit-body in construction. Ford introduces a special Starlift roof kit that was specifically designed to improve racing aerodynamics. NASCAR bans the kit after just one race. Ford's big-block grows to 406ci and receives cross-bolt main caps. Ford officially announces it will no longer follow the AMA ban on racing; Chrysler makes a similar announcement a short time later. The factory-backed NASCAR wars resume.

1963 Ford's big-block engine grows to a full 427ci, and the Galaxie line picks up a more aerodynamic "convertible" roofline at midyear. Chrysler introduces a 426ci version of the wedge engine, and Chevrolet brings out a short-lived, race-only powerplant called the Mystery Motor, the 427 MkIV. GM becomes nervous about its obvious violation of the AMA ban and completely withdraws from racing.

1964 Chrysler introduces the 426 Hemi engine, and NASCAR allows it to compete even though no street-going Hemis are produced. Ford protests, introduces the 427 High Riser engine, and threatens to unveil a single overhead cam version of the 427 big-block. Plastic glass is allowed in the rear window.

1965 NASCAR bans the 426 Hemi. Ford's High Riser 427 is banned at the same time. The Chrysler teams boycott the circuit until late in the season, when NASCAR allows Hemis back on short tracks. For the first time, a series-wide minimum weight of 3,900lb is established for Grand National cars. The maximum rim width is set at 8.5in for all Grand National cars. Holman and Moody perfects the rear steer suspension components that will be in use by most teams on the circuit for the next fifteen years.

1966 NASCAR allows Ford's single overhead cam 427 to run on the circuit, but only with a significant weight handicap. Chrysler's 426 is allowed in both full-sized and intermediate cars on all tracks.

Ford teams boycott the series. A driver's-side, four-sidebar roll cage is mandated by the rules book. The minimum weight rule is changed to 9.36 pounds per cubic inch. Bud Moore introduces a Mercury Comet intermediate race car. When Ford teams return to the fold late in the season, they too field "half-chassis" intermediates that have been fitted with 1965 Galaxie front frame clips. Deck lid spoilers are allowed on certain cars.

1967 Ford teams are allowed to field two four-barrel-inducted 427 Tunnel Port engines. The 9.36-pounds-per-cubic-inch rule continues, with a 3,500lb minimum weight now stipulated. Fuel cells become rules-mandated. Twin sidebars are required on the passenger's-side cage.

1968 Chrysler teams are allowed to run two four-barrel carburetors after FoMoCo drivers score four of the top five positions in the Daytona 500. In October, Dodge announces a more aerodynamic version of the Charger, called the Charger 500.

1969 Ford introduces a "rebeaked" Torino at the Daytona 500, called the Talladega. Two months later, a Mercury version of the Talladega, called the Spoiler II, is introduced simultaneously with the Boss 429, a hemispherically headed motor. Holley and Ford jointly introduce the 1,040ci Dominator carburetor. All Grand National cars are limited to one four-barrel carburetor. Dry-sump oiling systems are permitted. Front and rear spoilers are permitted. The rim width is expanded to 9in. A four-bar passenger's-side cage is required. After the Charger 500 proves incapable of dealing with FoMoCo's aero-cars, Dodge introduces a radically nosed and winged car called the Charger Daytona. A fully fabricated front chassis snout and upper control arms are permitted midyear. Some teams experiment at Talladega with an in-car radio system. Racing slicks are tried at the same race.

1970 Ford cuts its racing budget 75 percent. Plymouth introduces a renosed and bewinged Road Runner called the Superbird. Buddy Baker breaks the 200mph barrier at Talladega. Wheel size is expanded to 9.5in, a 12.1in sidewall width is established, and restrictor plates are introduced.

1971 Special aero-bodied cars are limited to 305ci. Chrysler cuts its racing budget to cover just two teams. Junior Johnson switches to Chevrolet, that manufacturer's first credible effort since 1963. The restrictor plate rule is changed to a carburetor sleeves rule. All side glass is outlawed. An onboard fire system is required.

1972 Chrysler withdraws from factory-backed racing. Restrictor plates return. Ford intermediates revert to full-frames with rear coil springs. Bud Moore builds a Torino powered by a 351 Cleveland small-block. The minimum weight is lowered to 3,800lb.

1973 Mark Donohue wins the Western 500 in an AMC Matador equipped with four-wheel disc brakes. Other teams soon make the switch to discs. Sealed ram air systems are outlawed.

1974 New small-carb rules for 7-liter engines cause most major teams to abandon big-block power once and for all. Dry-break fuel filler necks are permitted.

1975 Chevrolet introduces a new aerodynamic beak for the Chevelle line and calls the car the Laguna S-3. AMC terminates its factory racing support.

1977 NASCAR expands the three-year-body-style eligibility rule to four full seasons.

1978 NASCAR bans the Laguna S-3 nose.

1980 The minimum weight is set at 3,700lb.

1981 Downsizing reduces the wheelbase of a NASCAR-legal race car to 110in from the previous 115in standard.

1983 Ford introduces a newly redesigned Thunderbird that promises to offer greatly improved aerodynamic performance. Chevrolet brings out a new nose design for the Monte Carlo that replicates the one created by Ralph Moody for the Torino Talladega. Cale Yarborough drives a new Monte Carlo SS to a one-lap speed of 200.503mph in Daytona 500 qualifying, but demolishes the car on the next circuit of the track. In May, Yarborough qualifies for the pole at Talladega, with a 201.744mph lap in his Chevrolet—the first 200mph qualifying speed in NASCAR history.

1984 Cale Yarborough breaks the 200mph qualifying barrier at Daytona with a 500 pole-winning lap of 201.848mph. Three months later, his number 28 Monte Carlo sets a new pole record at Talladega with a hot lap of 202.692mph.

1985 Awesome Bill Elliott and his Ford Thunderbird begin their incredible year. Elliott ups the ante with a 205.114mph pole-winning lap. At Talladega, the sleek T-bird runs even faster: 209.398mph. In July, Elliott breaks the 200mph mark for the summer Daytona race, with a 201.523mph qualifying lap. Talladega gets even faster when Elliott blisters July, qualifying with a 207.578mph lap.

1986 Chevrolet and Pontiac answer Ford's aerodynamic advantage with two all-new aero-warriors. Chevy's T-bird answer is a bubble-backed version of the Monte Carlo SS, called the Aero-Coupe. Chevrolet's duplication of the Torino Talladega is complete. Pontiac tacks a droopy nose and a bubble-back window on the Grand Prix and calls the new car the 2+2. Undaunted, Bill Elliott runs 212.229mph in qualifying at Talladega. Summer Talladega speeds climb to 209.005mph with Elliott's help.

1987 Ford redesigns the Thunderbird and raises its bustle several inches. The car proves even sleeker than before. Bill Elliott runs 210.364mph in Daytona 500 qualifying. At Talladega, speeds climb to an all-time high: 212.809mph. The minimum weight drops to 3,500lb.

1988 NASCAR reintroduces the restrictor plate. Speeds drop to below 200mph at both Daytona and Talladega. Roof rails and side skirts are required following a horrific airborne crash suffered by Richard Petty in the Daytona 500. The Monte Carlo rounds out its racing career as the most successful marque in NASCAR history: ninety-five wins in 183 starts.

1989 Chevrolet's Monte Carlo replacement, the Lumina, is introduced. NASCAR reduces the restrictor plate size.

1990 The restrictor plate size is reduced to 7/8in.

1991 NASCAR begins to govern the spoiler angle in attempt to control speeds.

1992 A minimum 45-degree spoiler angle is announced. NASCAR limits front spoiler projection to not more than 1/2in beyond the front bumper.

---

the order of the day for most American auto manufacturers, and some car makes still mounted theirs transversely, in buggy fashion. The rules also mandated that lever shocks that shared the same equine origins be original equipment on some Strictly Stock sedans. Then, as now, live-axle differentials predominated. The gears that filled those third members usually reflected the general highway use that was their original mission. As a result, one problem that early racers confronted was finding gear ratios that were acceptable according to the rules and low enough for race duty. This was especially important on the short dirt ovals that characterized the early NASCAR circuit. Getting off the corners quickly often required a four-series gear—that is, a gear set with a ratio of 4:1 to 4.9:1—or better. Unfortunately, the freeway-minded two-series and low-three-series rings and pinions that most street cars came equipped with were, in many cases, all that was available. Truck gears were a solution for some, and in time, manufacturers interested in the sales that NASCAR wins could generate did begin to offer special optional "heavy-duty" gear sets. But initially, finding the right set of gears for a given track was a daunting task.

Though the dearth of high-performance stock suspension and drivetrain components that plagued early Strictly Stock teams was vexing, it wasn't the biggest chassis problem that confronted them; simple mechanical breakage was, and parts failure often sidelined most early Strictly Stock fields. It was the inability of stock parts to hold up to the wear and tear of racing use that ultimately both solved the lack-of-parts problem and moved sanctioning officials to permit the use of non-stock, purpose-built equipment that would go the distance.

Axle failure was a major problem for drivers during the first few years of the NASCAR circuit. This was an especially serious problem for Hudson Hornet drivers, since the small rear wheelhouses on their race car usually foiled a broken axle's attempt to escape from the differential. When that happened, the hapless driver and the car were usually sent into a series of end-over-end rolls that sometimes proved fatal. When it became clear to racers and NASCAR officials alike that a problem existed, the rules book was relaxed to allow all NASCAR race cars, regardless of make, to use the heavy-duty "floating"-style hubs and axles that had originally been installed on Ford trucks. Later, in the sixties, Holman and Moody (H & M), Ford's official Charlotte, North Carolina-based racing arm, refined that design, and the result is still in use under the current crop of Winston Cup cars.

Hudson's Hornet proved to be a successful car during NASCAR's first decade. All told, Hudson drivers won 79 races in five years of competition. Marshall Teague piloted his number 6 Hornet to back-to-back wins in the 1951 and 1952 Daytona beach course races. NASCAR Archives

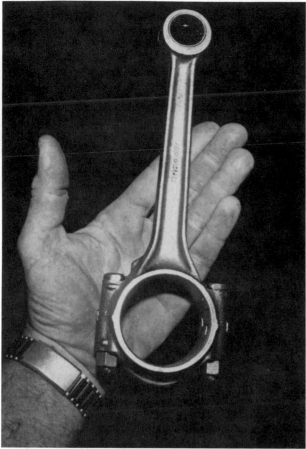

One reason for the phenomenal amount of torque churned out by a Twin H Power Hudson six-cylinder was its long rod length. The 308ci Hornet engines featured an undersquare 3.81x4.5in bore and stroke that produced enough torque to pull Amarillo to Anchorage.

Very little was changed away from stock in the interior of Pops Turner's 1956 convertible. Most of the original bench was still present, and so, too, was the bulk of the stock dash. Imagine going racing with that spindly looking three-on-the-tree shifter. The rudimentary roll bars of that era weren't very confidence inspiring, either.

The evolution of a Winston Cup car's brakes took a similar path. The narrow, small-diameter drum brakes that came as standard equipment on fifties-vintage American passenger cars were never intended to survive the rigors of dirt track or superspeedway racing. The heat produced by race work would often reach levels intense enough to boil brake fluid and warp structural members. When that happened, an early stock car became an unguided 4,000-pound (lb)-plus missile—with disastrous results. Little by little, creative interpretations of the usually brief official rules book led to rules-mandated changes that affected all competing cars. In the case of the brake system, drivers were first allowed to add to their cars ducting that was designed to direct cooling air to the often-red-hot shoes and drums. Next came the practice of "Swiss cheese" drilling a car's stock brake backing plates and then adding extra reinforcement plating.

In the sixties, Ralph Moody—one-half of the fabled Holman and Moody firm—developed fabricated "spiders" that replaced stock brake backing plates altogether. NASCAR officials subsequently allowed them to become standard equipment throughout the series. Wider, reinforced shoes with fully sintered metallic linings also came on-line during the late fifties and the sixties. Finally, the road racing team of Mark Donohue and Roger Penske persuaded sanctioning body officials about the merits of the aircraft industry disc brakes that had been standard fare in sports car racing for decades. The disc brake systems found today under Winston Cup Thunderbirds and Luminas are a direct evolutionary result of that change in the rules book.

The frame found under most early Strictly Stock race cars was usually—but not always—a standard, unboxed cross-member affair unchanged from its assembly line configuration. Some early competition cars—most notably the 1951-54 Hudson Hornets—did feature unit-body construction, but they were the exception rather than the rule. The earliest cars in the series raced with no, or at best only rudimentary, roll bars for driver protection, for example. Race preparation involved rolling down the side glass on the driver's side and then belting or wiring the driver's-side door or doors shut. Seatbelts were also not a uniform fixture in early Strictly Stock circles, and were usually Army Air Corps surplus when present at all.

As the series evolved, more attention was paid to safety, and this attention inexorably moved competing cars further away from the Strictly Stock formula. When the acrobatic proclivities of broken-axled Hudsons—and, to be fair, other makes—became evident, the rules book was changed to mandate some type of roll bar. In their earliest form, some of these "cages" had much in common with living room furniture—incredibly, some frugal drivers constructed roll bars out of hastily nailed together 2-by-4s, just moments before a race. However, increasingly stringent and specific rules evolutions saw first single metal hoops required, then four-point cages, then cages with one sidebar, and ultimately the life-saving cocoons that today surround Winston Cup drivers at speed.

Other alterations also found their way onto the underpinnings of a Grand National stock car. When shock absorbers of the day proved unable to last for the duration of a race, extra dampers were added to each wheel axle, first by add-on mounting towers and later as part

Wrecks were common and often catastrophic during NASCAR's formative years; many lives were lost. Lee Petty was lucky enough to survive the qualifying race trip he *took over the wall and out of the speedway prior to the 1961 Daytona 500. His number 42 Plymouth wasn't quite as lucky.* Rich Turner Collection

of specially fabricated sub-assemblies. Improved cooling packages, through-the-frame sway bars, fabricated control arms, and revised-ratio steering boxes all ultimately followed.

The full frames that supported the bodywork of most early NASCAR stock cars also went through their own evolution. Initially, few if any changes were allowed to a car's stamped-steel side rails and cross-members. During the first decade of NASCAR racing, boxing and rewelding began to be allowed to increase structural rigidity. The roll cage evolved from a single hoop to a multi-tube affair. The frame it worked in coordination with changed, too. As more and more changes were allowed, less and less of the original structure remained. Galaxie-derived front and rear "clips" came into wide use, and were accepted under the rules book for use on non-Ford cars as long as bits and pieces of the original frame rails were used to connect them. Ultimately, purpose-built tubular steel chassis that completely replaced all trace of a car's original frame were put into competition.

When the green flag fell on the first Strictly Stock race on June 19, 1949, at a 3/4-mile dirt track in Charlotte, each of the thirty-three cars on the starting grid sported stock, unmodified sheet metal; all their original side trim and brightwork; stock front and rear bumpers; and full roll-up windows. Over the next three decades, Grand National, nee Strictly Stock, cars lost progressively more of their stock bodywork, all their side trim, and just about all their factory safety glass. Modern NASCAR stock cars have fewer stock body panels and in most cases wear a collection of body panels that have been handmade from raw sheet steel.

Among the thirty-three competing cars that took part in the first Strictly Stock race, nine different manufacturers were represented. Three Lincolns (including the winning entry driven by Jim Roper), four Hudsons, six Oldsmobiles, two Buicks, ten Fords, two Chryslers, one Kaiser, and even one lone Cadillac all took part in that race. The engines that powered them during the 200-lap contest included flat V-8s; flathead straight sixes; flathead straight eights; and two versions of the first

Hornets were powered by low-revving flathead straight-six engines. What they lacked in horsepower, they made up for in torque—and that was exactly what was needed to get a car around the NASCAR dirt tracks of the day. When racers persuaded Hudson to fit Hornets with twin one-barrel carburetors, it was one of the first instances of direct factory involvement in stock car racing.

overhead valve V-8 engines to be produced by the Big Three (Ford, Chrysler, and GM), in the Cadillac and Olds entries. The rules of the day prohibited power-increasing modifications on any of the engines in question, except for the removal of the stock muffler. As a result, that first race, and the others that followed, represented a test of both the power output of a stock engine and the efficiency of the package it powered. In the early days of NASCAR competition, big wasn't always better, when it came to engine displacement—especially if the engine in question had to lug around two tons-plus of stock automobile. It was entirely possible, as a result, for a comparatively underpowered engine to perform well if not saddled with an excessive amount of avoirdupois. In fact, that's just the formula that Plymouth drivers like Lee Petty employed to win many early NASCAR races.

Other elements influencing the performance of early stock racing machines included the amount of torque an engine produced and the aerodynamic package that a given engine was assigned to propel. Strong performances in both of these categories helped torquey and bullet-shaped Hudson Hornets thoroughly dominate the NASCAR ranks during the first few years of the fifties.

Very shortly after the series made its debut, factory involvement sparked the beginning of a horsepower war

Ford referred to its first overhead valve V-8 as the Y-block. When introduced in 1954, it displaced 239ci and put out 130hp. By 1956, displacement had climbed to 312ci and power was an impressive-for-its-day 225 ponies. Ford drivers won fourteen events that season, second only to Chrysler's all-conquering twenty-two.

that reached its peak in the late sixties in the form of massive, semi-streetable 7-liter engines that were offered in street-going homologation cars solely to make them legal on NASCAR's high-banked ovals. The first salvo in this three-decade competition was fired by the Hudson company when NASCAR racers convinced the factory to build an engine with twin carburetors instead of the single one-barrel fuel mixer that had theretofore come as factory equipment. The new package was called Twin H Power, and it helped drivers like Herb Thomas and Marshall Teague win seventy-nine races between 1951 and 1955. Oldsmobile drivers had enjoyed an early advantage on the circuit owing to the all-new 135-horse 303-cubic-inch (ci) overhead valve V-8 engines (a first for cars from the General) with which their Futuramic 88 race cars came equipped. Atlanta's famous Flock brothers (Tim, Fonty, and Bob), Curtis ("Pops") Turner, and others won twenty of forty-one races in 1951 with their V-8-powered Oldsmobiles. When Hudson Hornet drivers began to steal their thunder, factory engineers released new racing gears that carried bona fide factory stock numbers, in 1952.

Other over-the-counter "heavy-duty" high-performance pieces—each also carrying a Regular Production Option (RPO) part number—began to show up in short order. In 1954, the brass at Olds, desirous of the publicity that racing victories bring, decided to make all the special cams, rear ends, and suspension pieces they had in stock retroactive in application to 1949.

Chrysler Corporation engineers and sales executives were no more immune to racing fever than their Oldsmobile and Hudson contemporaries. Though the first hemi headed engine to power a Mopar car was rated at a meager 180 horsepower (hp) when introduced in 1951, four years later, the same 331ci V-8s had increased in potency to 300 ponies. In 1954, engine output took another jump, to an impressive 355hp, when displacement was increased by another 23ci. Mercury Marine mogul Carl Kiekhaefer fielded a well-financed team of Chrysler letter cars for drivers like Buck Baker, Tim Flock, Fonty Flock, Speedy Thompson, and Frank ("Rebel") Mundy during the 1955 and 1956 NASCAR seasons. They dominated the series, winning forty-nine of the 101 races contested those two years. Kiekhaefer's fleet of Mercury Marine-sponsored Chrysler 300s often swept the top three places in a given race, and at times won as many as sixteen events in a row. Tim Flock and Buck Baker earned national driving titles as a result of their stints behind the wheel of a Kiekhaefer-backed Hemi Chrysler.

Ford, long a presence in the modified and 'shine car ranks, didn't enjoy the same early success as its Hudson, Chrysler, and Oldsmobile rivals in the Grand National series. Things began to look up for Dearborn partisans when Ford introduced an all-new overhead valve engine of its own called the Y-block in 1954. Though not exactly intimidating in 1954 trim—the 239ci engine was rated at just 130 horses—it wasn't long before engine size and power output were both significantly increased. Displacement grew almost immediately, to 312ci, and so, too, did the number of over-the-counter hop-up parts offered by the factory.

Ford openly set up a racing facility in Long Beach, California, and gave Indy 500 winner Pete De Paolo the job of winning races for the blue oval. To that end, Fo-

Chevrolet and Ford pulled out all the stops for 1957. When Chevrolet introduced a fuel-injected version of the 283 small-block engine, folks in Dearborn countered with this McCulloch-supercharged 312 that was rated at 300hp. Chevrolet homologated the Fuelie in the Corvette and Bel Air lines, and Ford built a handful of supercharged Thunderbirds and Fairlanes.

MoCo engineers burned tankersful of midnight oil creating new and more powerful engine packages. In 1957, Ford built a homologation run of 300hp McCulloch (the chain saw people) supercharged versions of the 312 Y-block. Age-old rival Chevrolet countered with a fuel-injected 283hp version of the overhead valve small-block V-8 it had introduced two years before, and Chrysler raised the horsepower to 390 with an optional version of the 300C.

Of course, talented NASCAR mechanics like Henry ("Smokey") Yunick, who joined the Ford team in 1957, were not sitting idly by while the factories waged their own regular production battles. Working with—and sometimes outside—the sketchily written NASCAR rules book, NASCAR mechanics used their acumen to push power output well beyond what the factory claimed. Yunick, for one, had always taken a creative view of the sanctioning body's official rules and regulations. According to his interpretation, if a modification wasn't specifically forbidden by the rules book, then it must be legal. And in addition to the tendency of many NASCAR tuners to "stretch the envelope" a bit by bending the rules, more than a little downright cheating took place. The end result was more and more horsepower, and significantly increased racetrack speeds.

Of the factory-backed Grand National stock car teams, Ford enjoyed the most success in the late fifties. Money was spent on both new race cars and behind-the-scenes structure. Pete De Paolo, working with Ford liaison Joe MacKay, signed on John Holman, a skilled machinist and former truck driver for Lincoln's Carrera Panamericana rally team. Holman, in turn, hired name drivers like Ralph Moody, Curtis Turner, Glenn ("Fireball") Roberts, and Joe ("Little Joe") Weatherly. Even Chevrolet stalwart Smokey Yunick was persuaded to join the Ford ranks in 1957. Combining the driving talent and mechanical skill of De Paolo's team with the

Ford teams came on like gangbusters in 1956, both in Grand National competition and in NASCAR's sibling convertible division. Curtis Turner drove a factory-backed Sunliner to twenty-two dirt and asphalt wins that season. NASCAR Archives

The car makers were taking a more active role in racing by the mid-fifties, and special equipment designed solely for NASCAR competition began to show up as RPOs. Mercury, for example, offered a twin four-barrel–equipped 335hp engine package that was clearly designed with competition in mind. This Bill Stroppe–prepared Montclair driven by Tim Flock sports twin shocks and air bag coil spring assists. Mike Slade

high-performance hardware that was rolling off the Dearborn assembly lines put Ford in a position to win. Though Ford drivers had visited NASCAR victory lanes only three times between 1949 and 1955, in 1956 and 1957 they dominated the series and won forty-one of the 108 races held.

This caught the attention of GM executives like corporate president Harlow H. ("Red") Curtice. Realizing that continued Ford success on the NASCAR circuit would undoubtedly cut into Chevrolet's market share, Curtice knew that GM would have to counter Ford's stepped-up racing program with one of its own. But that created a problem, since GM was more than a little worried about possible antitrust legislation the federal government might be considering against the car-manufacturing giant. Although increased corporate sponsorship of NASCAR racing might counter the Ford threat, it would also likely bring unwanted attention from the federal government. Curtice solved this dilemma by getting the Automobile Manufacturers Association (AMA) officially to ban factory-backed automobile racing. Sensing trouble ahead, NASCAR officials took the parallel step of outlawing any engine not employing a single four-bar-

Mechanical Specifications of the Top Five Cars of NASCAR's First Decade

Car Type	Engine Type	Displacement (ci)	Horsepower	Curb Weight (lb)	Wheelbase (in)	NASCAR Wins
1949-59 Oldsmobile	OHV V-8	303.7-324.3	135-202	3,455-3,707	119.5-122	85
1951-54 Hudson Hornet	Flathead L6	308	145-170	3,530-3,620	124	79
1955-59 Ford Fairlane	OHV V-8	272-352	182-300	3,155-3,916	115-118	70
1955-59 Chevrolet	OHV V-8	265-348	162-280	3,140-3,458	115-117.5	60
1955-56 Chrysler 300 Hemi	OHV V-8	331.1-354	300-355	4,005-4,145	126	49

Official 1950 NASCAR Rules Book

The official NASCAR rules book has always been a pliable and perplexing creature, in part because of its brevity. During NASCAR's first decade, the "official" rules book could be contained on a single sheet of paper. As a result, it had gray areas and loopholes that were large enough to drive a nineties-style team hauler through. Certain requirements were specified, but many more weren't.

It was that lack of specificity that permitted freethinking car builders to inch their Grand National cars further and further away from stock. Changes were made to the chassis configuration to improve handling, modifications were made to the engine to extract a few more horsepower, and additional safety gear was installed to better protect the driver. In some cases, these modifications were made clandestinely, just to see what the NASCAR inspectors would say. In other cases, changes to a race car's trim were made in concert with the sanctioning body. In either case, if a particular alteration was permitted on one car, it often began showing up on every other car in the garage area, as soon as the next race on the circuit. Over time, these changes became institutionalized and standard operating practice—often a part of the next "official" NASCAR rules book if the sanctioning body deemed them beneficial to racing.

Of course, what NASCAR giveth, NASCAR can—and often does—taketh away. The forty-year history of the sport is replete with examples of the sanctioning body's willingness to countermand, contradict, and just plain outlaw official rules and regulations that had been in effect as recently as the race before.

What follows is pretty much the entire 1950 Grand National rules book. As you read through it, imagine that you are the mechanically creative type and are looking for ways to improve the performance of your "stock car" within the letter—if not the spirit—of the rules. You should have very little difficulty coming up with dozens of ways to bend the official 1956 rules book to suit your own purposes. For certain, mechanics like Smokey Yunick and Ralph Moody did!

1950 Grand National Stock Car Rules and Regulations
NASCAR Grand National Championship circuit races are open to 1946 through 1950 models of American made passenger cars only.

1. All cars must have complete bodies, hood, fenders, bumpers and grilles.
2. Headlights must be removed or covered with masking tape.
3. Chrome or other parts may be protected by masking tape.
4. Windshield may be protected by celluloid or cellophane covering.
5. Rear seat cushion must be removed. Front cushion must be intact and not altered.
6. Muffler must be removed.
7. Doors must be strapped shut.
8. Radiator dust screens will be permitted.
9. Any wheel or tire size will be permitted.
10. Only stock radiator and cooling system will be permitted.
11. Water pump impellers may be altered.
12. Transmissions must be stock for model car used.
13. Differential must have stock catalogued gears for model car used.
14. Locked rear ends will not be permitted.
15. Overdrives and two-speed rear axles will be permitted.
16. Complete motors must be in chassis and body for which they are catalogued.
17. Bore may not exceed .030 oversize and stroke must be stock.
18. Valves, valve springs, cylinder heads and manifolds must be stock.
19. T-3 Ford camshafts or altered camshafts will not be permitted.
20. Ignition system must be stock.
21. Flywheels must be stock. No alterations permitted.
22. Carburetor jets may be of any size.
23. Shock absorbers may be adjusted or valves changed only. No other changes permitted.
24. Any fuel and oil will be permitted.
25. Pickup in fuel tank may be moved to right side.
26. Any type spark plugs will be permitted.
27. Self-starter must be in working order.
28. Removal of fan or fan belt or air cleaner is not permitted.
29. In all of the above specifications the word "Stock" shall be defined as meaning any part which is listed in the manufacturer's catalog for the year, model and type car entered.
30. No Jeeps, suburbans, station wagons or pickups will be permitted.
31. It is recommended that wheels, hubs, steering parts, radius rods and sway bars be reinforced and strengthened in any manner.

Dirt tracks were common on the Grand National circuit during the fifties. One of the most famous was the 4.1-mile combination beach-and-road course in Daytona where both Grand National Division and convertible division cars tore up the sand and asphalt every February. NASCAR Archives

Though all the major manufacturers were officially out of racing in 1958, battle lines were already being drawn for the factory-backed stock car wars ultimately waged during the sixties. Holman and Moody prepared for the coming fray by building independently backed race cars for
paying customers. Pops Turner and Little Joe Weatherly were two of the early NASCAR stars who drove Holman and Moody– prepped cars during the fifties. NASCAR Archives

rel carburetor, effectively eliminating Ford's supercharged Y-blocks, Chevrolet's Fuelie 283s, and Chrysler's 8-V-inducted Firepower Hemis.

Ford executive Robert S. McNamara—later the Kennedy administration secretary of defense who believed he saw light at the end of the Vietnam tunnel—swallowed Curtice's manipulation of the AMA, hook, line, and sinker, and pulled Ford out of racing. The factory-backed teams were disbanded, and their parts were either sold or given away. John Holman and Ralph Moody took advantage of the pullout by using much of Ford's leftover inventory to set up their own race shop in Charlotte. GM made a show of closing down its racing operations, too. Lee Petty wound up with most of the high-performance Oldsmobile pieces the factory had produced, and Ray Nichels took home the special Pontiac parts. Production of hotted-up Chevrolet race components was supposedly stopped at the same time. Funny thing was, though, the bow-tie division's backdoor never seemed to swing all the way closed.

As NASCAR's first decade came to an end, the major factories were officially out of the racing business. Even so, racing continued. And, as things turned out, the short-lived GM-engineered AMA ban ultimately set the stage for the now-famous factory-backed racing programs of the sixties and early seventies.

In its first ten years of existence, NASCAR had evolved from a regional series based on strictly stock automobiles to one centered around competition cars that were increasingly removed from showroom configuration. Sanctioning body rules still required regular production origin for most of—but not nearly all—the hardware that went into the construction of a Grand National race car. But the political, mechanical, and financial forces destined to transform Big Bill France's Strictly Stock series into a venue for purpose-built, hand-fabricated "silhouette" cars were already in play.

Stock car racing gained stature and prestige when Bill France opened the Daytona International Speedway in 1959. The 2.5-mile high-banked oval was unlike anything the stock car racing world had ever seen. Craft Collection

Smokey Yunick: Testing the Rules

Few names are as strongly associated with the early days of NASCAR stock car racing as that of Smokey Yunick. Tagged with the Smokey moniker during his days as a Penn State motorcycle racer—on a semi-oil-tight British mount, of course—Yunick was interested in the internal-combustion process early on.

Flying Fortress duty in the Army Air Corps during World War II both whetted Yunick's mechanical appetite and set him on the path to his legendary status as a race car builder and tuner. His high-altitude work also led him to the then-small town of Daytona Beach, which, during training mission fly-overs, struck him as a pretty nice place to live.

Once hostilities were suspended, Yunick moved south to the Sunshine State and set up shop just a few blocks from Daytona's fabled white-sand beach. Yunick's self-proclaimed Best Damn Garage in Town very quickly became the congregating point for the speed seekers who came to test their mettle on the flat white-sand land-speed-record course that was exposed at every low tide.

When fellow Daytona Beach garage owner Bill France conjured up something called NASCAR, Yunick was one of the series' first competitors. It didn't take long for his mechanical ability and creative interpretation of the official NASCAR rules book to make the cars he constructed the class of any field they graced. First associated with the Fabulous Hudson Hornets that dominated the Strictly Stock ranks in the early fifties, Yunick later shifted his allegiance to General Motors cars and that mammoth corporation's number one racing advocate, Semon ("Bunkie") Knudsen.

In the fifties and sixties, the trademark black-and-gold Pontiacs and Chevrolets that Yunick built on the surface plate [a fixture for precisely aligning a chassis] in his Beach Street shop were regular features both on the track and in victory lane. During that time, just about all the name NASCAR and US Auto Club (USAC) drivers of the day spent time in the cockpit of a Yunick-prepared stock car. Herb Thomas campaigned Hornets for Yunick and then helped him score the first win for Chevrolet's new small-block engine in the 1955 running of the Southern 500 at Darlington, South Carolina. Marvin Panch put a Yunick-prepped Pontiac in victory lane at Daytona in 1961 to notch Yunick's first win in the 500, and the late, great Fireball

Smokey Yunick was an influential and innovative mechanic. In NASCAR's first two decades, he campaigned cars for most of the major car makers. The list of stockers he built includes Hudson Hornets; small-block Chevy–powered One-Fiftys; Super Duty Catalinas; Mystery Motor Impalas; 427 Chevelles; and swoopy, Boss 429–powered Torino Talladegas. NASCAR Archives

Roberts backed up that win with another the following year. Curtis Turner drove a series of controversial Chevelles for Yunick during the mid-sixties, and that duo's sparkling performance led to the legendary stories about Yunick's 15/16-scale and "extra-gas"-capacity Chevrolets.

Yunick's Chevrolets also played host to a number of USAC stars. "Lone Star J. R.," Johnny Rutherford, drove a Mystery Motor-powered Impala in the Daytona 500 for Yunick in 1963, for example. Bobby Unser, Anthony Joseph ("A. J.") Foyt, and Gordon Johncock also spent time at the helm of cars that had been built in Yunick's garage.

In 1969, Yunick followed his corporate mentor, Bunkie Knudsen, to Ford and, as a result, took an active part in the factory-backed aero-wars that were waged between FoMoCo Talladegas and Mopar winged cars that season. However, Knudsen was sacked by Henry Ford II shortly before the 1970 NASCAR season, and his departure from the manufacturing scene also effectively marked the end of Yunick's active participation on the circuit. Even so, Yunick remains a fixture both in Daytona Beach, where he lives in semi-retirement, and in NASCAR circles, where his mechanical advice is still sought by many racers.

Yunick graciously took time away from developing his reverse-dynamometer project (a device intended to measure the parasitic losses suffered by an internal-combustion engine while rotating), writing his regular column for Circle Track Magazine; and fielding the technical questions posed on the constantly ringing phone in his shop, to provide some insight into the earliest days of stock car racing.

Q.—What did you do to the chassis of the cars back in the Hudson Hornet days? Did you leave them completely stock, or modify them in some way for racing?

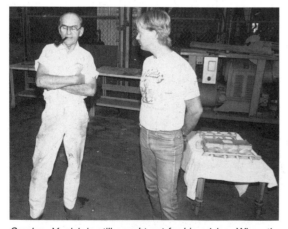

Smokey Yunick is still sought out for his advice. When the NASCAR circuit returns to Daytona every year, his Beach Street garage is a popular stop for many crew chiefs.

A.—Well, I started with the thing in 1946, and we weren't allowed to do anything. We could run any camber setting that you wanted. We couldn't move the axle. Couldn't do anything about wheel bearings. Couldn't do anything about wheels. So we couldn't do anything.

The very worst problem we had was tires. They wore out, and we had no tires. The only tires available were those that were sold by the only manufacturer. There wasn't any such thing as stock car racing tires. There wasn't for a long time. Some bought tires from Champion and some from General. Unocal back then was called Pure Oil. They had their own tire—they actually made a tire. It wasn't a brand-new tire, because each of the manufacturers had their own tire facilities. They hired an engineer to work for them who was a racing tire authority. So he did a little work. Pure Oil was marketing them at Pure Oil gas stations. Pure Oil put a couple bucks into the early racing effort. Pure Oil's tire was better. Some people would run that.

Engine inspection as it was, they always told you what you couldn't do. We weren't allowed to do anything. We had a lot of axles breaking, and we had to run stock axles. In the inspection, they would search for part numbers. With axles like that, they had numbers on them. They would al-low cab "A" frames. They had numbers on them. The numbers were stamped on the metal, and we painted over them. They didn't spend a lot of time checking part numbers on wheels. We weren't allowed to reinforce them in any way. We weren't allowed to widen the rims, and we weren't allowed to change the offsettings.

We took the stock shocks off, and we ran aftermarket shocks. When we first started in modifieds, some of us were still running friction shocks. Most of them were some sort of hydraulic shock that had oil going inside it. They'd make you check them to see if you did anything to the inside of it. There was no such thing, back in those days, as having the perfect shock. You had a situation where if you broke an axle, the wheel came off. If you broke the hub, the wheel came off. That's how it was—you couldn't do anything.

A lot of guys drove their race cars to the race and then took the back-up plates and the headlights off, took the windshield wiper arm off, wound both windows down on the left side, took a strap and wrapped it around the roll bar—which was supposed to be one of the few add-on parts in it. In some cases, the roll bar was 2-by-4s nailed together right at the racetrack. You couldn't run without some kind of

Chevrolet sat on the NASCAR sidelines until 1955 when the all-new 265ci small-block engine was introduced. Smokey Yunick quickly put the new, free-revving little overhead valve V-8 to work in the Grand National Division. Herb

Thomas drove Yunick's Motoramic One-Fifty to victory in the 1955 Southern in Darlington, and this photo captures the celebration. It was Chevrolet's first NASCAR win; more would follow. NASCAR Archives

a roll bar, so some guys would get the 2-by-4s and cut them off and nail them together inside the car. We would get some wire or cable or something, and wrap it around them. Lots of cars ran with the license plate on them.

We weren't allowed to take any upholstery out. In the beginning, if you had a full front seat, you weren't even allowed to take that other front seatback out.

Q.—What were the first changes NASCAR allowed teams to make?

A.—The first concession, they made on the inside: you were allowed to take the back off the front seat because before, you had to run a full front seat. What changed it [our ability to make modifications] was the problems we were having. Because if we broke something, we were out of the race or someone got killed. When a Hudson Hornet broke an axle, the wheel would be stuck, and you'd flip. The fender would always go into the rim. Like, maybe three out of five of them did that. Wheelbearings. We just couldn't do anything. When they broke, sometimes you'd have a real serious injury, or what would happen was, by the time the race was through, or almost over, there might be four or five guys left running, and all the rest of them were out.

So then they started the rule changes. For example, if a particular manufacturer offered a heavy-duty hub, a heavy-duty spindle, and a heavy-duty axle, we were allowed to run them. So by this time, we were running modified. To make the rear end safer, we started using a 1-ton Ford truck rear end that had a hub that would run on two bearings. That ran on the axle shaft itself. The axles were one-piece and had a big flange. So the rules were changed to allow a full-floater rear end. Then it became mandatory to have one type of rear end and that type of hub. You weren't allowed to run without it. That took care of the back part. In the front, we were allowed to make sleeves to bolt on our spindles, to decrease the diameter of everything. Of course, they were made out of steel. Back in the first part of it [the series], we were operating pretty much on leaf springs. We had leaf springs in the front and [transverse leaf springs] in the back. Some of them still had independent front axles. And then we went to coils at the front and got rid of the straight axles.

Q.—How did you prepare a car for track duty in the Strictly Stock days? From what you've said, it sounds like the very first cars, you just drove to the track and raced. You really didn't make any mechanical changes.

Smokey Yunick still has the 265 block that powered Herb Thomas to victory in the 1955 Southern 500. Note the front-style engine mounts and the screw-in plugs located in the timing chain valley.

A.—Well, yes, the Hudson Hornet stock springs were mostly leaf springs. So most of us learned how to make the springs on our own. We changed leaves and changed spring eyes, but mostly we played with the arch of the springs. We made our own springs. We produced them. In the beginning, we couldn't add any leaves. Then they allowed us to. One problem we had was that every car back then had solid front axles and leaf springs. Later they got independent suspension and coil springs. Rubber bushings were a problem, too. Those things would get beat up, and the rubber got worked out of the front end. We'd be out of alignment on account of we'd pick up 3/8in of clearance with the rubber knocked out. In those days, when you worked the front suspension, we had a lot of trouble with the idler arms. So they restocked the factory and made the heavy-duty ones that we could use. Finally, they would allow you to reinforce the A-frame and pretty much do whatever you wanted to do. But they didn't let you change the offset and all that. In other words, you could only take a stock A-frame and make it stronger.

Heading towards handling, it was all a cut-and-dried situation. We were hindered by the rules. In other words, it wasn't a deal where somebody new could come in, that was a front man, and re-engineer the front suspension. None of us competing knew what was going on. What most guys did was move the spring rate. And when they allowed us to put more than one shock on, they added other shocks. The shock deal was very stiff. And the spring deal was different. In other words, to turn these things into a race car, the first thing we had to do was put heavier springs on, whether they were coils or leaves, then heavier shock absorbers, and then add another shock.

Later, with time, the modified suspension, the hub in front, and better wheel bearings, hub breaking and the rear axle breaking were all going away, but we were still breaking wheels. It was a very slow evolution. It was like a string that NASCAR held and slowly let it out and gave us a little more latitude towards getting things to be reliable. In other words, in the beginning, very little attention was paid to getting the spring rates and shocks right. All the rest was based on survival.

Q.—What could you do with the chassis itself? It's been said that very early on, you paid attention to the underside of the car for aerodynamic reasons. Is it true that you put Bondo on some of the open frame rails to smooth out the airflow under the cars you campaigned?

A.—Yes. What happened was, when I first started doing this, the real truth is, none of us knew what the hell we were doing. We learned as we went. Some of the things that happened to me at the beginning were a surprise. [I had just] come out of the Air Force, where I flew four years, and I was very aware of aerodynamics. It was part of my living. The aerodynamics were something they never bothered with in the rules book, so then they started allowing a lot of the changes, and I started getting braver and braver underneath. We built a deal that you could put a car on and pick it up and spin it. That made it easy to work on the undercarriage. I just kept adding more and more to it, and they didn't do anything. So I started changing the roofline and most of the windshield.

[Bill] France didn't suspect anything, and in '68, I had a Chevelle [frame] that was made out of channel iron. It was light in the front and had A-frames that were adjustable. We built our own frame out of cheap steel so it would be lighter and yet stronger and so on. And when I got to inspection with it, they threw it out and said, a) First, replace the homemade frame with [a] stock frame, [and] b) replace all the suspension with stock suspension. You could take the stock A-frame at that time and cut it in sections and shorten the length. That was all right. But you weren't allowed all the other things.

Q.—How about tires? How important were they in the early days of stock car racing?

A.—We had a terrible time with tires at first. I had a job with Chevrolet in '55 to build a Chevy and run at Darlington. I think the idea was for us to learn more about stock car racing. Our job was to win the race with Chevy, to help Chevy switch young people to buy the cars.

I figured racing with Chevy was more or less a hopeless case. I figured we were short on speed. We had 265in, and the others were like 310. So after I took the job, I thought about it and decided the only way to win the race was the tortoise and the hare thing. So I sent Mauri Rose off to find me some tires. He was very familiar with tires, not only here in the United States but in Europe as well. So he asked what he could do. So I said, "The best thing you could do for me would be to go find an 18in tire that's pretty well made, 'cause the only hope we have to win the race is tires. We don't need to have any tire problems if we're short on speed." I estimated we'd be short about 3mph. The rule book had a tire width, and you couldn't run slicks. We had tried to run recapped slicks, but they weren't any good on the asphalt, and they (NASCAR) stopped us.

Mauri called from Akron, Ohio, in a junkyard and said, "I think I've got the tires you want. But I've got to do something about it in the next hour. I'm at a junkyard in Akron, and they've got 170 of these tires, but they're getting ready to burn them." They made their own electrical power there, I think, and the tires were fuel. They were a very special tire that Firestone had built for Richard Cunningham to run at Le Mans. These tires were 16in, and they had a special trademark on [them]. It was called Super Sport. Not only that, they were whitewall on one side. They were 16in non-directional tires. So I said, "Where are we at?" Mauri said, "Well, this guy wants to mess with me with these tires. We have to buy them now, or they'll burn them." So I said, "What other leads do you have?" He said, "Nothing. I've got nothing on 18in." No one's ever seen anything in 18in except those tall truck tires. No one was willing to change them to make a reasonable tire for you. So I said, "All right, buy them."

When they first brought the first cars to the race, there was 680 tires blowed that day. Everywhere you looked, there were tires all over the racetrack. It got to the point where they couldn't stop the race often enough to move the caps. They just kept on going. As you went by, you moved over, and the next time you moved over, and so on.

Q.—Who was responsible for the heavy-duty hubs at Holman and Moody that became standard equipment on all stock cars in the sixties?

A.—Well, they [Holman and Moody] were. See, by this time, we were making the hubs out of 4130. It was a very expensive process, all the way around. We got rear ends and then used truck axles, and we cut the ends off the axles to make our own deal and weld them on.

Q.—Who was the first person to come up with the idea of the heavy-duty hubs?

A.—I would have no way of knowing who was the first person. We went from stock hubs to heavy-duty hubs that weren't working, and stock spindles to heavy-duty spindles which weren't working, and stock axles to heavy-duty axles which weren't working. The minute that they would turn us loose, then we would just machine moly hubs.

I don't remember which end we worked on first. I think the rear end first. Of course, it solved the Hudson Hornet problems. So what I did was take a half-ton Chevy pickup axle and made the ends out of 4130, bolted them on, weld-

Smokey Yunick was one of the earliest car builders in the NASCAR ranks to start using screw jack–adjustable coil spring perches. The 1962 Super Duty he built for Fireball Roberts (Number 22 here) was equipped with screw jacks at all four corners, for example. Roberts drove that black-and-gold car to victory in the Daytona 500 that year, finishing just ahead of a fresh-faced Richard Petty (43). Rich Turner Collection

Early race cars like Fireball Roberts' Catalina used fairly primitive screw jacks; they were really little more than large-diameter bolts that applied pressure to the top of each coil spring. Crude add-on shock towers were also the norm in 1962.

ed flanges on them, and they made hubs for them. We had a lot of troubles with the lug nuts, so we made our own lug nuts and lug bolts.

So I made my own stuff. But at Holman and Moody, you went in there and got the big, thick kind. See, the GM axles we were running at the time really didn't have enough rear end in them to be reliable against a Pontiac. You had a very poor selection of gears. When Holman got going, we got a very broad selection. They made a nodular piece where they eliminated all the negatives in the rear end. And so, when that happened, we switched over to Ford, and NASCAR allowed it. That was around 1961. The main reason they accepted it was because of the gear selection, because on half-mile tracks, none of us could get low enough; 5.4 was as low as we could go, and sometimes even that wasn't enough—and the cars were heavy then, over 4,000lb.

Q.—The current NASCAR rules book specifies a race weight of 3,500lb. How was race weight set during the early years of the sport?

A.—How that worked was, every fall time of year, all racers would go to all the different showrooms—Ford, Chrysler, Chevrolet, Lincoln, Olds 88, and so on, to look for the lightest car that fit the rules, that had the strongest engine. So the whole thing was cut-and-dried.

Q.—Winston Cup cars today have specially fabricated and fully adjustable underpinnings that are far from stock. One of the unique features of a modern stock car's suspension is the screw jacks that allow each individual wheel to be adjusted during a race. Who was responsible for that innovation, and when did screw jacks show up in NASCAR?

A.—I know we had screw jacks for a long, long time.

Q.—Do you know when? Was it '62? The Catalina you built for Fireball Roberts that year had them, didn't it?

A.—Well, we had them in '59, I know that. That Pontiac had screw jacks on it. Not only did it have screw jacks, but it had [a] hydraulic adjuster on top of the right front coil, and also had automatic height adjustment on the front, power steering, and power brakes.

Q.—That was all legal then?

A.—It was for a couple of races, until they outlawed them. In '59, I was racing then. The steering felt good going into the corners, but it was too slow or too fast on the straight away. It was all over the place. What the problem was, was that you had ahold of a steering wheel that was really big, and if you let go with one hand to change position to get a better grip, it would spin out of your hand, and then you had a hell of a time grabbing it back. But if you drove it like this, [hands at 10 & 2—Ed.], then you could only go this far. Well, maybe that wasn't enough. Those things jumped all over the place. To jump two car widths over was nothing. Tony Bettenhausen said, "You'll never hit the wall. The air will pick you up and hold you off. I guarantee you'll never hit the wall. Leave it alone. Don't try to correct it. It won't go into the wall, and if you turn it the other way, you may end up in a ditch."

That '60 Pontiac had air jacks on it, but I had to take them off.

Q.—Air jacks like they are using in Formula One and CART pit stops today?

A.—Air jacks. At Darlington, when we made a pit stop, the car just jumped off the ground. Thirty minutes later, they made me take them off.

So I don't know who the first guy was, but I assume that power steering, power brakes, and air jacks and screw jacks might have come out of this shop. I didn't know what the other guys were doing. I never paid any attention to what Bud Moore or anybody else was doing. I just figures that my contest was between Mother Nature and the racetrack. We'd get the car out there, we'd run around that racetrack and run the distance. If that happens to be second-best in qualifying, we might be running at the end for the first 100 miles. Then, after the race was getting half over, I might adjust that up or down.

I always operated with the idea that the race, for us, didn't start until we got down to the last 75 miles of a 500-mile race. We didn't need to race anybody until we got to the last 75 miles because it was pointless to me to race someone who wasn't going to be there in at the end. You just tried not to get lapped. If there was someone who was really dominant, then it was really foolish to try and race them, to push your car that hard. You just make up your mind you can't get it done today and aim for the top five.

Q.—What things could—or did—you do to the cosmetic trim of a car, to make it more aerodynamic?

A.—We did a lot of work underneath the car. We learned about spoilers and started using them. Like that car that's up in Childress' museum, I think the front bumper is wider-than-stock.

Q.—You mean the '66 Chevelle you built for Gordon Johncock to drive in the '68 Daytona 500?

A.—We stripped the front off of it. Cut the bumper in

During his racing career, Smokey Yunick often stretched the official rules book like a rubber band. In 1968, it finally broke when he tried to get this 1966 Chevelle past NASCAR inspectors. The list of things they gave him to change before the car could run began with, "Remove frame and replace with stock unit." Needless to say, the Chevelle didn't make it into the starting line-up. It did, however, become part of NASCAR racing lore.

half, welded a 2in strip to it, straightened it, and pounded it and put it back. Maybe 6in back from the front of the bumper, we'd have a spoiler down there. They wanted it 3in from the ground when you went through inspection. There'd be a couple of nuts, and you'd drop it down for the race. The same thing in the back.

Sometimes we'd raise or lower the deck lid. The windows were pushed out so pressure couldn't build. We played a lot with offset weight, trying to get the car as light as it could go. People would say, "What are you doing that for? It still has to weigh 3,900lb." Well, if we could get 300lb on the left side of the frame, that would help.

Q.—How did NASCAR check for weight distribution in the early days? Was it like today, where only a percentage of a car's weight can rest on its left wheels?

A.—Yes, but they didn't weigh from front to rear. So we did play around with weight. We moved the steering column as far to the left as we could. The driver was practically in the door. And then we'd lower the driver so we could get a lower center of gravity.

Q.—Tell us about the evolution of the stock car engine. In the early days, you had to run bone stock. When did NASCAR allow you to make changes, and what changes did you make?

A.—At first, we could only make the same changes the factory did. Like the Hudson, we only had a one-barrel carburetor until the factory bolted another one on for racing. Later Oldsmobile introduced a special cam that they built in a couple cars. Except for that, the engine had to be bone stock.

Our way around that was to start playing with the lobe centers on the cam, even though we had to run a stock profile. We got away with that for a long time, then they got wise to that. By that time, the factory started making some pretty good cams. Maybe they wouldn't actually build the engine with the thing, but they put the cam kit in the trunk. They had a part number for it, but they didn't install it. Ford made a lot of specialty pieces and heads, too. And after that came the big engine.

In the sixties, they [the engines] started getting bigger and bigger. Like the Talladegas. Everything I worked on was based on like 430in, plus all the parts, that engine was considered 500in. The next might be 10in bigger, and the next 20in bigger. It wasn't a deal where they could have gotten much bigger.

And then the lights went out on big engines. The Mystery Engine [1963 Chevrolet Mystery Motor] was a good engine, but it was too big. The 427 was a piece of shit. They were both one and the same engine, but the guy who designed them had to keep the bean counters happy. And when they got through fixing the cost, they changed the cylinder heads, changed the valve arrangement, [the] combustion chamber got changed, [the] ports got changed, it got less bore and more stroke; and the valve's gear angle got changed, too. At that time, we dealt with a 427 small-block. It was about 550hp. I would never have opened up the small-block, and no driver wanted a 427 big-block. What the problem was on the little block, after you got past 2000[rpm], you flat run out of cylinder head.

So the engine development was... everybody worked on it to begin with, and everybody thought the secret of winning races was power. It had a lot to do with it, but what was more important was—we was running on a half-mile dirt, mostly—torque, a lot of low end torque, not top end power. The big thing back then was more and more lift on the cam. Every one [cam] was wilder than the one before. The guys who were getting it done were working on cams that would get off the corners good. They were winning races. Almost none was working on torque. They all wanted wide-open horsepower and more and more radical cams. They should have been working on bigger ports. Well, they could have used bigger valves, too.

Q.—What about the transmission? Now everyone is running either an evolution of the Ford top loader or a modified BWT-10. Were stock transmissions required in the early days?

A.—Well, when we first started, we had to run the transmission that came in it [the car]. If you had [a] model of Chevrolet, there were no other options. That was it. What happened later was that all the race cars started to use Ford rear ends and Ford transmissions. Holman and Moody were making that rear end available for a reasonable price. Then Ford introduced the top loader, and that got to be a way of life.

Q.—What can you tell us about brake evolution? Stock brake drums and shoes were required by the rules in the forties and fifties, were they not?

A.—Yes. Brakes got bigger in diameter. Brake drums got heavier and stronger, and brake shoes got larger. Material got more and more effective and more exotic. Everything put together was everything known to man. Brakes

One of the items NASCAR officials took umbrage with about Smokey Yunick's Chevelle was the fully adjustable and fully fabricated upper control arms that he had created and installed. Handmade A-frames weren't allowed on the circuit until 1969.

got big, and then they OK'd discs.

Brakes were a serious problem. They got big, and we had a hell of a time with brake fluid and heat. You spent 20 percent of your time working on the brakes. Probably the biggest single thing that helped us was the use of iron, fully metallic brake shoes. Before them, brakes would probably last only 200 miles in a race. After they came about, we had brakes for just about double that. Of course, we still had a problem with heat. Heat would boil the brake fluid and warp the backing plates. We spent many hours trying to cool the things off. We drilled the backing plates, for example, and we ducted air to the brakes from outside.

Q.—When did NASCAR first begin to permit the use of larger-than-stock brakes? Was it during the fifties?

A.—Oh, no. When did the first Riverside race take place? It was around then.

Q.—That was in 1963. Was that about the time that the Holman and Moody-developed big drums came into widespread use?

A.—Yes, that was standard. The real wide shoes that we tried to use first didn't work. They would go out under stress. The shoe would deform and just leave a line where the central rib was. Then we started to add bracing to the underside of the shoe, and that more or less solved the problem.

Q.—Driver safety has certainly come a long way since the forties. You mentioned the 2-by-4 "roll cages" that some drivers nailed together in the early days. What do you recall about the evolution of safety equipment in the early days?

A.—Well, at first, guys would go out and buy Army Air Corps surplus seatbelts and bolt them in. We found out that lap belts were good. But a shoulder harness in a Hudson Hornet would kill you. The only good weapon a driver had against getting killed was to lay down. With [a] shoulder harness, you couldn't. We went to Atlanta, and a guy got killed because he couldn't lay down. Two of them got killed. One in a Hornet. He broke an axle and went end over end and couldn't lay down because of the shoulder harness. So we took them [shoulder harnesses] back out.

And then we started putting in roll cages. We welded them to the frame, roof, and to the door frame. Nobody paid much attention to the seat, so we started putting a bar across the lowest part and angled the seat to put a bar up behind it. We went back to a shoulder harness and put a release on it for emergencies. If it got locked up, the driver could pull on a little handle and release it. Once the roll bars were in the cars, it solved the problems. Then we started putting bars in diagonally.

Q.—How about onboard fire systems? When did they come into use?

A.—Well, we had one. I wasn't impressed with the fire extinguisher, and later they mandated them. If you had a fuel cell, you didn't have to worry about fire. The only fire you had to worry about was from the oil pan.

Q.—That brings up the question of fuel cells. We've heard that you were one of the first car builders to install them. When did that happen?

A.—In '63. Chevys had a tank way in the back. If you looked at the back of the race car, you saw this tank hanging out the back of it. The gas cap door was right in the middle of the tank. Every time you got hit in the ass, you'd knock the cap off and gas would come out and there'd be a fire. Later, [in 1964] when Fireball [Roberts] got hurt, I said I'd never race a stock car again without a fuel cell. I was fooling around with helicopters at the time, and they had fuel cells, so I had an aircraft supplier make up a 22gal cell for one of my race cars. NASCAR wouldn't let me run it at first, though

Significant Car of the Period
Carl Kiekhaefer's Chryslers

Mention the name Chrysler and you're likely to flash on the image of a block-long boulevard cruiser that has been stuffed full of every sybaritic creature comfort known to the Western world. And, truth be known, Chrysler cars have pretty much been aimed at the blue-blood-and-blue-rinse market niche for most of the past three decades. Still, at one time, the marque had a dedicated working-class following and genuine racing credentials that were hard won on the NASCAR circuit.

In 1955, Chrysler luxury cars first began to show up at NASCAR-sanctioned events. Their presence on those racing grids was directly attributed to one man's decision to test the Grand National waters. Carl Kiekhaefer was his name, and his decision to enter the rough-and-tumble world of the dirt track "bullrings" was based on a coldly calculated business decision rather than a deep-down love of motor racing. As the owner of Mercury Marine, a manufacturer of outboard boat motors, Kiekhaefer was interested in promoting his products directly to the consumers most likely to buy them. When market research identified the typical NASCAR race as a natural gathering place for potential Mercury Marine customers, Kiekhaefer jumped into the Grand National circuit with both feet.

The cars he selected to serve as rolling billboards for his company were all examples of Chrysler's famed letter series, which made its debut in 1955. Designed from the start with racing in mind, Chrysler letter cars were basically two-door versions of a normally sedate New Yorker that had been treated to a dose of mechanical steroids. The 300Cs that drivers like Buck Baker, the Flock brothers (Bob, Fonty, and Tim), and Speedy Thompson first campaigned for Team Mercury Marine boasted the United States' first non-supercharged 300hp regular production engines. The 1,725 model 300Cs that were built that first year of production also featured revised underpinnings that were designed to eliminate a stock New Yorker's tendency to wallow in the corners like an elephant kneeling for its mahout. Chrysler 300s were intended to provide rock-solid, luxurious high-speed transport—both on and off the track. And they did.

In 1956, Chrysler engineers turned up the underhood heat a notch by offering a 354ci high-compression version of the hemispherically headed overhead valve V-8. Built on Chrysler's marine assembly line to closer tolerances than those of regular road-going engines, the new Hemis featured forged internals, a solid lifter, long-duration camshafts, and twin four-barrel Holley induction. When installed ahead of a heavy-duty three-speed manual transmission and mated to the upgraded handling package standard in the letter series line, these engines afforded spectacular performance.

But mechanical superiority wasn't enough for the methodical Kiekhaefer. Like some contemporary car owners, he left no stone unturned in his pursuit of racing victory. First he assembled a "superteam" composed of the best drivers that his estimable amount of money could buy. Next he outfitted the team with enclosed car haulers—unheard of in those days of drive-your-race car-to-the-track competition—and then he attended to every detail that might affect the team's success. Meteorologists were consulted, for example, about race day weather conditions, and team cars were prepared accordingly. Extensive test and race records were kept of track conditions during testing and previous races, for the same reason. Kiekhaefer even went to the

Outboard boat motor manufacturer Carl Kiekhaefer thought NASCAR sponsorship would be a good way to promote his product line. Unfortunately, the Great White Fleet of 1955 and 1956 Chrysler 300s he prepared for drivers like Fonty Flock and Buck Baker was too successful for its own good.

Instead of inspiring sales, the 49 Grand National victories the cars scored—dozens of which often came in a row—only aroused ire. They also gave NASCAR officials and race promoters more than a few sleepless nights. Mike Slade

Carl Kiekhaefer's 1955 and 1956 Chryslers were powered by twin four-barrel–inducted 331ci and 354ci hemi-headed engines. In stock trim, they were rated at 300hp and 355hp, respectively. Mike Slade

NASCAR rules in the fifties allowed few changes away from stock. Original equipment bench seats were mandated, for example, and only their passenger's-side back could be removed. Notice the full dash instrumentation and column shifter. Mike Slade

extreme of having the dirt surface of various tracks on the circuit analyzed to help determine the optimum race day setup.

Kiekhaefer's belief in thorough preparation sometimes bordered on obsessiveness. He had strict rules about driver "fraternization" the night before a race, for example, and would house husbands and wives on opposite sides of a hotel. Even so, that preparation paid off in spades during the 1955 and 1956 seasons, in which he nearly brought the new NASCAR circuit to its knees by winning so many events that fans grew angry and bored and stayed home in droves. Of the 101 events contested those two seasons, Kiekhaefer Chryslers won fully forty-nine. At one point during the 1956 season, the troika of Buck Baker, Tim Flock, and Speedy Thompson won an incredible sixteen straight races.

Though repeatedly "torn down" postrace by NASCAR tech officials, Kiekhaefer's cars were always found to be within the rules of the day. And so, the victories stood, much to Bill France's consternation.

Just as Kiekhaefer had entered the NASCAR series based on a calculated business decision, he left the circuit in 1957 for much the same reason. When it became obvious that continued racing success would alienate rather than endear potential Mercury Marine customers, Kiekhaefer shut down his operation as abruptly as he had begun. The dominance his Great White Fleet of Chrysler letter cars enjoyed and the back-to-back national titles they earned for drivers Tim Flock and Buck Baker are little more than a memory for even the most avid contemporary fan. Even so, it can be said that the professionalism Kiekhaefer brought to the sport during his brief time on the circuit was a harbinger of the total dedication and thoroughness that are necessary to score victories on the Winston Cup circuit today.

Chapter 2

Redefining 'Stock': The Sixties & Seventies on the Circuit

NASCAR's first decade came to a close with all the major car manufacturers ostensibly out of racing—but that doesn't mean competition was lacking on the track. In fact, the first shots in the horsepower war to be waged during the sixties were already being fired on the NASCAR circuit.

Early Horsepower Wars

Though out of racing owing to the AMA ban, Ford introduced an all new "big-block" engine family in 1958, referred to in-house as the FE series. The hottest version was a 352ci overhead valve V-8 that sported a solid-lifter cam, a single four-barrel carburetor, and a 10.6:1 compression ratio. The new engine was factory rated at 300hp. Though that was no improvement on the power output a Y-block 312 was capable of, the potential of the new design was far greater than that of Ford's original valve-in-head V-8.

Ford was not alone in the new engine department. Chevrolet powertrain engineers had also been hard at work on a big-block engine of their own. As introduced in 1958, the new bow-tie division's motor displaced 348ci and was rated at 280hp. It, too, had been designed with plenty of room for growth—in both displacement and power output. Not to be left out of the big-block club, Plymouth trotted out a wedge-headed large-displacement engine that was called the Golden Commando. The new V-8 featured an octet of cylinder bores that added up to 350ci, and was rated at 305hp. Pontiac, Oldsmobile, and Dodge countered the trend toward big-block engines with hotted-up powertrain packages of their own based on existing engines.

Before the end of the decade, cubic inch figures and horsepower ratings were crowding the 400 mark in all the major American car lines. These engines quickly began to show up on the NASCAR circuit, and racing speeds continued to climb—regardless of the AMA ban.

Aside from the introduction of new regular production engines, each of the major auto makers responded to the AMA's edict in its own way. Ford, under Robert McNamara's guidance, took the prohibition most seriously and got out of racing, even detuning the 352 engine that had been designed before the ban. Pontiac, at the command of inveterate racer Bunkie Knudsen, curbed its racing program the least. The Indian head division continued openly to manufacture and sell high-

performance hardware that gave Poncho drivers a decided advantage over the competition in short order. Chrysler and Chevrolet fell somewhere in between the two extremes. Though not openly racing, both continued to develop engine and drivetrain parts that were clearly intended for racing use. Chrysler labeled its work "law enforcement" related, and Chevrolet took a similar tack. The bow-tie people also kept the backdoor of their research and development (R & D) department wide-open, clandestinely keeping loyal Chevy racers well stocked with go-fast goodies. While Ford engineers twiddled their thumbs, Chevrolet introduced new four-speed transmissions, a 6-V induction system for the 348, and a wide variety of other horsepower gear.

The results of these varying responses to the GM-engineered AMA ban quickly showed up in the NASCAR record books. In 1957, Ford dominated the

Ford introduced an all-new big-block engine family in 1958, called the FE line. Though original displacement was just 332ci, that figure quickly grew to a more robust 427ci. As the engine line evolved, it picked up features like beefy cross-bolted main journals, an improved side oiler lubrication system, and even multiple carburetion. Horsepower ultimately exceeded 600 in race tune.

Grand National Division, winning twenty-seven of the fifty-two races held. Chevrolet drivers were just no match for the Ford juggernaut that year, especially during the first half of the season, before the ban went into effect. All told, it captured only eighteen checkered flags—fourteen of those after the ban. Things were completely different just one year later when Chevrolet pilotos like Fireball Roberts, Buck Baker, and Speedy Thompson won twenty-three events to Ford's sixteen. Things were much the same in 1959, with Ford drivers having little success against the triple team efforts of Chevrolet, Oldsmobile, and Pontiac that prevailed in twenty-nine of forty-two events.

John Holman and Ralph Moody tried to stem the GM tide with a fleet of 430ci big-block-powered Thunderbirds that had been driven through loopholes in the rules book and Ford's normal procedure for buying parts. Holman and Moody was a wholly independent firm in 1959, and not officially associated with the Ford factory. Nevertheless, contacts still existed between the two, and Holman and Moody used these to buy a number of "scrapped" 1959 Thunderbirds that had not made it successfully off the Wixom, Michigan, assembly line.

Once it had the cars in its Charlotte facility, the H & M crew set about turning them into Grand National-legal stock cars. The new and larger Thunderbird line that had made its debut the year before featured unit-body construction and coil spring suspension at all four corners—both firsts for a Ford race car. When fitted with the optional 350hp 430ci Lincoln engine, the cars were a formidable package despite their 4,200lb curb weight. Holman and Moody-prepped Square 'Birds, as you might suspect, offered even more performance. Racing modifications conducted by H & M's T-bird Power Products Division included beefing up the suspension with heavier spindles, brakes, and reinforced control arms; installing a four-point diagonally braced roll cage; replacing the factory carpeting with an asbestos mat; adding seatbelts and shoulder harnesses; bolting in a 22gal gas tank; and hooking up a tachometer. Ready to run with a race-tuned 430, an H & M Thunderbird went out the door for $5,500—a considerable sum of money, in 1959, for a race car.

Ford shut down Holman's "scrap" supply of Thunderbird chassis as soon as Robert McNamara got wind of it, and NASCAR wasn't too keen on the idea of allowing such a big engine in a car that was significantly smaller than the competition. Even so, eight Holman and Moody 430 'Birds were ultimately built and campaigned. In fact, Ralph Moody was given the honor of being the first to lap Bill France's new superspeedway in Daytona in a race-spec H & M Thunderbird.

Although Holman and Moody's fleet of Thunderbirds provided a Ford presence on the Grand National circuit, their drivers proved unable to match the success of Chevrolet, Olds, and Pontiac drivers who were still receiving direct, if unofficial, factory support. As the season progressed, accusations began to fly between the major auto makers, about violations of the AMA ban. By the middle of the 1959 season, it was clear that Ford was the only car manufacturer actually following the AMA's ban to the letter. Movers and shakers at the home office in Dearborn were justifiably aggrieved about that fact, and on April 27, 1959, a letter was sent to General Motors stating Ford's intention to reintroduce performance options of its own. The letter also called for a reworking of the AMA ban.

When GM failed to respond, it was the beginning of the end for the AMA ban. Shortly thereafter, Ford formed a group of three engineers to work on the same type of "law enforcement" parts that GM and Chryco had been turning out during the previous two seasons. When it came time to test the endurance of those new police pursuit parts on an actual racetrack, it would have seemed natural for Ford's former factory rep Holman and Moody to get the assignment. But that would have been too obvious. Instead, the lesser-known Wood Brothers, of Stuart, Virginia, were selected for the testing assignment, and Ford was back—though not quite openly—in the racing game.

Things went pretty much unchanged in the General Motors ranks for 1959. Though 348 big-block power was available in new Batmobile-finned Impalas, most bow-tie racers still chose to run the lighter 1957s that were still legal. Fireball Roberts and Cotton Owens campaigned full-sized Pontiac Bonnevilles, and Lee Petty continued to field Oldsmobiles—at least for part of the season. In March of 1959, Petty rolled out a couple of 350-powered 1959 Plymouth stockers that he used on and off for the rest of the season. The two extra cars allowed Petty's son, Richard ("King"), to drive his dad's spare 1957 Olds 88s at selected races during his debut season on the circuit. By 1960, both would abandon their Oldsmobiles altogether, effectively eliminating that GM division from representation in the NASCAR ranks.

The rules book that governed Grand National stock car competition in 1960 had grown considerably from the one-page affair of just ten years before. The provisions it contained were significantly more specific, yet at the same time they allowed more deviation from stock than ever before. Stock body panels and bumpers were still required, and so was a stock frame, but NASCAR mechanics were allowed great leeway in most other areas. Side glass was optional, for example. Many internal engine choices were now left up to the builder's discretion as well. Full-floating axles were the norm. Air bags were permitted to augment coil spring rates, and the use of multiple shocks at all four corners became optional. Manufacturers also were given the freedom to introduce special speed-related parts—if 1,500 similar examples were made available to the public. The word *Stock* in NASCAR's name was becoming more and more of an abstraction.

Ford, Chryco, and GM continued to turn up the heat on the NASCAR circuit during the first few years of the sixties, while all were supposedly still working within the AMA's guidelines. Following Robert McNamara's departure to "mastermind" JFK's—and later LBJ's—Vietnam "police action," Ford formally re-signed Holman and Moody to head up its racing efforts early in 1961—just as they were preparing to go Dodge racing. The 352ci big-block engine finally grew the extra 38ci it had been intended to before the AMA ban, and in hottest trim it was rated at 375hp. Ford dealers began to stock over-the-counter gear sets in ratios all the way to 5.83:1. Four-speed Borg-Warner T-10 transmissions also became an option that same year. In 1962, Ford's biggest engine grew another 16in, to 406in, and by year's end had picked up a beefy cross-bolt main journaled bottom

When the squared-off-roofline found on 1962 Galaxies proved to be an impediment to racetrack performance, Ford introduced a new "convertible"-rooflined Galaxie in the middle of the following season. Fireball Roberts was one of the Total Performance Team drivers who drove the sleek new Galaxies to twenty-three victories that year. Mike Slade

end. A three-deuce manifold and hotter cam took that engine over the 400 advertised horsepower threshold to 405hp in street trim.

In a move that was more than a little predictive of factory behavior in the late sixties, Ford even introduced special body parts designed specifically to improve the aerodynamics of the Galaxie line. The kit in question was an attempt to improve on the boxy, squared-off roofline of the 1962 Galaxie. Ford introduced a swoopy liftoff roof panel that was designed to bolt onto a Galaxie convertible's body. Referred to as the Starlift package, the new kit was basically a reprise of the swoopy roofline that had been stock on 1960 and 1961 Starliners. Though Ford took pains to display Starlift-equipped cars at various dealerships and in official parts catalogs, the pure racing nature of the new lid was pretty obvious. When in place on a convertible body, the new roof made it impossible to roll up the car's rear side glass, for example. And, of course, removing and installing the bulky roof panel in your home garage would have been quite a chore.

When Holman and Moody showed up with two Starlift-equipped Galaxies at the Atlanta 500, NASCAR tech officials were perplexed. Ultimately, both Nelson Stacey's number 29 and Fred ("Fast Freddy") Lorenzen's number 28 Fords were allowed to compete. Lorenzen went on to win the race, only to have NASCAR officials declare the victory illegal and ban the special roof panel post-race.

Though the Starlift roof had little effect on the 1962 season, it did precipitate a formal announcement from Henry Ford II about Ford's full return to factory-backed racing. When asked about the company's position on factory-backed racing, the day after Lorenzen's "victory," Ford replied:

"The so-called safety resolution adopted by the AMA in 1957 has come in for considerable discussion in the last couple of years... I have a statement to make on the subject.

"I want to make it plain that I am speaking in this instance only for the Ford Motor Company. I am not speaking for the AMA, of which I am currently president, or for the other manufacturers.

"Following the adoption of the AMA resolution, we at Ford inaugurated a policy adhering to the spirit and letter of the recommendations contained in the resolution. We tried very hard to live with this policy. We discontinued activities that we felt might be considered contrary to the principles embodied in the resolution and also modified our advertising and promotion programs appropriately. For a while, other member companies did the same. As time passed, however, some car divisions, including our own, interpreted the resolution more and more freely with the result being that increased emphasis was placed on speed, horsepower, and racing.

"As a result, Ford Motor Company feels that the resolution has come to have neither purpose nor effect.

Fireball Roberts' 1962 Catalina was powered by an "over-the-counter" Super Duty 421 engine that was not available from the factory as original equipment. Even so, it *was legal for use on the NASCAR circuit owing to its "stock" part number and availability to the buying public.*

Accordingly, we have notified the Board of Directors of the Automobile Manufacturer's Association that we feel we can better establish our own standards of conduct with respect to the manner in which the performance of our vehicles is to be promoted and advertised."

Chryco entered the big-block engine wars in 1958 with a 361ci engine referred to as the Golden Ram. By 1962, engine displacement of that wedge-headed series had increased to 413ci, and street-going versions sported cross-ram induction.

In other words, Ford was officially getting back into factory-sponsored motorsports competition. Chrysler soon followed suit.

General Motors and Chrysler engineers had been as hard at work on horsepower improvement in 1960 and 1961 as their Ford counterparts. Chevrolet punched out its 348 to a fine 409ci in 1961, and installed it in a perimeter-framed Impala that was over 200lb lighter than the year before. First-year 409 engines were factory rated at 360hp, and that was increased to 409hp just one year later. Corporate cousin Pontiac introduced an "over-the-counter" dealer-installed 421 engine in 1961, to power its Catalinas, and by the following year, NASCAR mechanics reportedly had that engine producing in excess of 465hp in racing tune.

Chrysler's answer to the new GM and FoMoCo engines was to introduce successively larger versions of the B engines that had come on-line in 1958. By 1962, displacement had grown to 413ci, and the engine sported an elaborate cross-ram assembly that placed each of the four barrels far out over the valve covers at the end of long runners. Free-flowing exhaust manifolds worked in concert with the radical induction setup to produce an advertised 375hp in street trim.

Larger and more radical engines were just around the corner for all three manufacturers. Before the middle of the decade, each would introduce engines that moved 7 liters of air with every rotation, and cranked out more than 425hp in the process.

The year 1962 was a phenomenal one for GM drivers on the Grand National circuit—and none were more successful than those fortunate enough to be driving Wide Track Pontiacs. Fireball Roberts accomplished the impossible by winning the pole position for the 1962 Daytona 500, the 100-mile qualifier race for the Thursday before the main event, and the race itself, in a black-and-gold Smokey Yunick-prepared 1962 Catalina. By season's end, Poncho drivers had visited twenty-one of the other victory lanes on the circuit.

The fourteen wins turned in that year by drivers of 409-powered Impalas, like Rex White, were more than arch rival Ford's six checkered flags but not nearly enough to cause Catalina drivers any discomfort. Something more would be needed in 1963 to close the gap— and that missing something was horsepower. Taking a leaf from Pontiac's "nonregulation production" engine book, Chevrolet engineers began to work on an all-new polyangle valve big-block engine. It came to be called the Mystery Motor, owing to the secrecy in which it was shrouded. Based on all-new castings, the engine featured a unique four-bolt bottom end with two-piece main caps, a high-revving oversquare reciprocating assembly that displaced 427ci, and a pair of "porcupine valve" head castings that incorporated equally spaced ports and large valves. Pre-season test sessions at desert proving grounds with the new motor were so impressive that Pontiac drivers and crew chiefs like Junior Johnson and Smokey Yunick immediately began making plans to field Mystery Motor-powered Chevrolets in 1963.

Car construction began while Chevrolet engine foundries were still casting up the requisite number of new 427s to complete the season. All signs seemed to be pointing to another season of GM domination on the NASCAR circuit—this time, by Chevrolet drivers—until just weeks before the running of the Daytona 500 in February of 1963. Though Mystery Motor work had been conducted with at least the tacit approval of Chevrolet's top brass, when word of the all-new race-only motor began to leak out to the motoring press, someone far up the chain of command got cold feet. Chevrolet was, after all, still supposedly honoring the 1957 AMA ban on factory racing that had been engineered by its chief executive. And there was still the worry that too much publicity might bring federal antitrust investigators down on the corporation.

Whatever the motivation, several weeks before the 1963 Daytona 500, Chevrolet contacted each of the teams that had received some of the forty-odd 427s that had been cast—to ask for them back. As you might imagine, that recall was met with little enthusiasm and more than a little invective. Ultimately, the teams that had already received Mystery Motors were allowed to keep them. But Chevrolet made it clear that not one more part would be available—either over the counter or out the backdoor.

In the week before the running of the 500, Junior Johnson's white number 3 Impala and Smokey Yunick's black-and-gold number 13—driven by a painfully young looking Johnny Rutherford—were the class of the field. Both easily won their 100-mile qualifying races, and Johnson shattered the record books with a 165.183mph lap of the 2.5-mile superspeedway during practice. Unfortunately, the limited R & D work the new engines had

Like all Grand National cars of its day, Junior Johnson's number 3 Impala carried most of its original brightwork into battle.

received prior to Chevrolet's decision to shut down the program had failed to detect a serious problem in valvetrain reliability. As a result, none of the Mk IV-powered Impalas finished the race. (Mk IV was Chevrolet's official name for the new engine.) Persistent mechanical failures would continue to dog Johnson and members of the other Mystery Motor teams for the rest of the season. By the end of the fifty-five races contested that year, Johnson had exhausted his supply of spare parts and, in fact, was campaigning a 427 that Holman and Moody had acquired in an attempt to prove that the Mk IVs weren't really available to the general public. When John Holman had asked to buy a Mk IV at a local Charlotte dealership, Chevrolet had decided to provide one to avoid the creation of even more negative publicity.

Though Ford drivers swept the first five places in the 1963 Daytona 500, the lightning-fast Mystery Motor Impalas still raised embarrassing questions about adherence to the AMA ban. The result of those inquiries ultimately led to the abandonment of motor sports participation by all the General's divisions, at midyear. Chevrolet's backdoor—and Pontiac's—had finally been bolted shut. Grand National competition was effectively a Ford and Chrysler show for the next ten years—but that doesn't mean it was boring.

With the General's legions on the sidelines, the stage was set for a titanic battle between Chryco and FoMoCo for NASCAR wins. The engines and chassis components that each of the giant car makers developed during the first few years of the sixties would ultimately influence the sport until the nineties.

Chassis and Suspension Wars

In fact, the underpinnings of the current batch of Winston Cup "stockers" aren't all that far removed from the suspension components that were found under Fred Lorenzen's Holman and Moody-prepared 1965 Galaxie. Like full-sized Fords in the fifties, the Galaxies that graced NASCAR starting grids during the sixties all began life as full-framed regular production cars. By 1963, Holman and Moody had become a veritable racing factory and was the point of origin for just about every Ford in the typical NASCAR "show." Construction of a Grand National Galaxie got under way with the deliv-

Here is the basic Holman and Moody chassis circa 1963. Stock Ford Galaxie frame rails were used, and so, too, were reinforced Galaxie control arms. The through-the-frame exhaust dumps were outlawed by the 1964 rules book.

ery of a body-in-white chassis (so called owing to the white sheen of its unpainted bodywork) that had been pulled from a regular production assembly line shortly after receiving all of its body panels, but before the installation of sound-deadening, drivetrain, or interior components.

Once the Ford chassis were in-house at H & M's sprawling Charlotte airport complex, the first order of business was the rewelding and gusseting of all stock frame seams and joints. A multipoint roll cage was added next. In the early sixties, the NASCAR rules book only called for a two-hoop, four-point affair that carried but a single sidebar. As the decade progressed, diagonal braces and an increasing number of sidebars were required.

When Ford racers shifted to smaller, unit-body Fairlanes in late 1966, Holman and Moody developed a half-chassis snout that was used to replace those cars' stock shock tower front suspensions. The new frame member consisted of rewelded 1965 Galaxie rails and fabricated spring perches. It was connected to a Fairlane tub by two long rails that ran inside the rocker panels. The same basic design has been in use ever since. Though fabricated frame rails replaced the Galaxie units in mid-1969, an H & M half-chassis' suspension mounts and geometry are still being used under "rear steer" cars today.

NASCAR abandoned its requirement that a chassis front snout be based on factory stampings, in 1969. From that point until the present, series stockers have featured fully fabricated front frame members nearly identical to the snout found in this 1969 H & M Talladega.

Full-chassised Galaxies in 1965 became the model for most Ford, Chevrolet, and American Motors (AMC) Grand National stock car suspensions. (That's right, Rambler did go racing—in the seventies.) The suspension mounting points, frame geometry, and frame rail spacing found under the fleet of Galaxies that Holman and Moody built in 1965 all became standard in the typical NASCAR garage area. In fact, these can still be found today at the bow of cars that still feature rear steer 1965 Galaxie worm-and-sector steering boxes and attendant steering gear (front steer cars are based on Camaro componentry and geometry). Even after NASCAR officials permitted the use of add-on snouts in the unit-body Ford cars that came on-line late in 1966, reinforced stock Galaxie front clips were used. Later, in the middle of the 1969 season, the rules book changed again to permit the installation of fully fabricated snouts. Even so, 1965 Galaxie frame geometry and layout were still part of that frame design.

A similar evolution took place with the suspension components that bolted to the frame itself. In the early sixties, only stock upper and lower control arms were permitted. No modifications of any kind were allowed except for changes in wheel alignment specifications. As the years progressed and the speeds increased, NASCAR inspectors slowly permitted more and more alterations away from stock in the name of safety.

As time passed, those modifications became more extensive. Both control arms were boxed for greater strength, for example. Towers were added to the frame adjacent to the control arms, to serve as mounting points for extra shock absorbers—and, in some cases, the Air Lift air bags that were occasionally used to augment spring rates. Heavy-duty coils were part of the program, too, as were beefed-up tie rod ends, strut rods, idler arms, and other steering gear. Power steering was not permitted in the series—though Smokey Yunick had tried it on Marvin Panch's 1961 Daytona 500-winning Pontiac—so H & M Galaxies used an unassisted assembly line-style box to dial in steering changes.

At first, front chassis adjustments were achieved solely by altering spring rate and height and changing

The Car That Made Richard Petty King: The 1966-1967 Plymouth Satellite

You might say Richard Petty had a natural advantage when it came to stock car racing. His dad was, after all, an early star on the NASCAR circuit. When young Petty decided to follow in his dad's burnt rubber footsteps, it was only natural that he would take to the high banks in one of the senior Petty's race cars.

But once behind the wheel, the young Petty quickly made his mark. By 1964, he was a Grand National stock car star in his own right and an important weapon in Chryco's NASCAR arsenal. However, it wasn't until 1967 that Petty began to be called the King of Stock Car Racing. The car that made that ascension possible, Petty's all-conquering 1967 Plymouth Satellite, is on display in the Joe Weatherly Museum in Darlington.

Based on a body-in-white Plymouth intermediate that was delivered to Petty Enterprises just prior to the 1967 season, King Richard's GTX was based on a unit production chassis that had originally been "bucked" on a regular production Plymouth assembly line. Once in-house at Petty Enterprises in Level Cross, North Carolina, the car received the full NASCAR treatment. At the bow, that meant first reinforcing the stock snout and then adding a tubular upper loop that tied into a multipoint roll cage that was fitted to the driver's compartment. Tubular upper control arms that took the place of the RPO A-frames and mounts were added to accommodate two shock absorbers for each wheel. In keeping with the erstwhile stock nature of

Grand National competition, stock-style torsion bars were retained, but significantly stiffer rates than stock were employed. Large-diameter drums and fully metallic segmented shoes rounded out the front suspension and acted upon stamped-steel 15in rims that carried treaded Goodyear stock car specials.

The rear suspension on King Richard's 1967 was also quite similar to stock in configuration. Built around a bulletproof 8 3/4in corporate differential, the GTX rode on a third member that was suspended by leaf springs and housed a set of track-specific gears. As at the bow, a quartet of shocks was used to control jounce, and two more drumdisc combinations scrubbed off speed.

Motive force was provided by a firebreathing 426ci Hemi engine that was mated to a corporate four-speed transmission. Breathing through a single 1 11/16in four-barrel Holley carburetor and a set of flat collector headers, the King's Hemi cranked out in excess of 600hp. That was enough to propel the not-so-svelte 3,900lb stock car to velocities in the 175mph range on the big tracks.

Petty took in the superspeedway sights from within a gutted control cabin fitted only with the essentials needed for going fast. A single reinforced production bucket seat placed him behind a stock-style dash that had been equipped with a brace of analog gauges. A multipoint roll cage assembly took up most free space but did permit easy access to the four-speed shifter and the thickly wrapped stock-style steering wheel. Directional inputs were not power assisted, and the brake pedal received its only motivation from Petty's right leg. The hard work of manhandling

The year 1967 was the one in which Richard Petty was crowned King of Stock Car Racing. The car that made that coronation possible was this Hemi-powered number 43 GTX. Petty won an incredible twenty-seven of forty-eight races entered that year, and at one point visited victory lane ten straight times.

This is the 426 Hemi engine that made Richard Petty both King of Stock Car Racing and a two-time Grand National Championship winner in 1967. The fabricated "front loop" had become standard equipment under the hood of a Grand National stock car by the middle of the sixties. It served both as a safety device and as the mounting point for suspension components. It was tied into a reinforced snout derived from stock frame rails.

King Richard Petty's "throne" during the 1967 season was a reinforced van seat that placed him behind a tape-wrapped stock steering wheel and a gutted dash. A Hurst shifter jutted from the bare floor nearby. Safety equipment was minimal: just a handheld fire extinguisher and a quick-release safety harness were all Petty had to keep him from harm's way.

onship. He'd also picked up the now-familiar title of King of Stock Car Racing.

When asked about his phenomenal 1967 season and the car that made it possible, Petty is characteristically modest. According to him, his 1967 GTX was "just another car. I never really had a love affair for that particular car. It was really not an outstanding car." Perhaps that's the way it seems to the King of Stock Car Racing, from his 200-race-wins viewpoint. The official NASCAR record book paints another picture of the car entirely.

the car around the tracks on the circuit was made all the more difficult by the full roll-up side glass that racers relied upon for aerodynamics. Interior temperatures in the 130-degree-Fahrenheit range were not at all uncommon, and Petty often lost 10lb in fluid weight in a single sitting.

The sheet metal panels that housed the whole package were also strikingly stock in appearance, though perhaps not exactly in fact. The NASCAR rules of the day did not permit many obvious modifications. Wheelwell openings were altered to permit easier tire access during pit stops, for example, and headlight openings were allowed to be covered over, too. Cheating up the car—as Petty calls it—for superspeedway work involved things like pulling in and lowering the fenders as much as possible in an attempt to cheat the wind.

In final form, Petty's electric blue 1967 Plymouth was a formidable package. When the season began, he quickly served notice of that fact by winning eleven races before the midpoint running of the Firecracker 400 in Daytona. Immediately after that July 4 race, Petty stunned the racing world by going on a rampage that's not likely to be repeated. He won five more races in four weeks before embarking on a two-month-long winning streak in August that saw him park his Plymouth in victory lane at ten straight events. By season's end, Petty had racked up an incredible twenty-seven wins and his second Grand National driving champi-

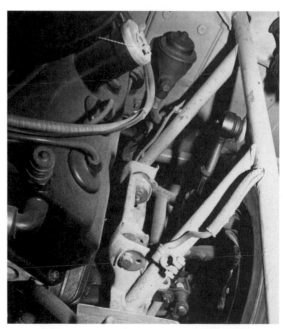

As in all Mopar race cars of the era, the front suspension in King Richard Petty's GTX consisted of fabricated control arms, two shocks for each wheel, and twin torsion bars. It was a complicated system to set up and adjust.

Fred Lorenzen's 1967 Holman and Moody Fairlane was typical of the unit-body cars that Ford racers turned to following the factory's boycott in 1966. The cars were built around half-chassis snouts that had been grafted onto the bulk of their unit bodies. The 1967 Fairlanes were built more than a little on the boxy side, but they were small, and that made them much more nimble than the lumbering Galaxies that they replaced. Lorenzen's Galaxie did not feature any aerodynamic add-ons, and even sported its original door handles and windshield trim.

the car's alignment setting, up to the 4 degrees of negative camber that NASCAR allowed. For a time between 1960 and 1962, NASCAR also allowed the use of the auxiliary Air Lift air bladders that had come into use during the late fifties. Ultimately, those Air Lift bags were replaced by a screw jack assembly that placed the top of each front coil in a cup that was independent of the rest of the chassis. The amount of weight supported by each spring cup was adjusted by turning a fine-thread bolt mounted in the spring perch.

The identity of the innovative mechanic responsible for coming up with this arrangement has been lost to history. Early NASCAR-related literature mentioned Jack Sullivan, Fireball Roberts' 1963 Holman and Moody crew chief, as the screw jack's originator, but that seems to be at odds with the finding of similar equipment on Smokey Yunick's Wide Track Pontiacs years earlier. Dick ("Hutch") Hutcherson, a midwestern racer and owner of a race car fabrication shop, recalls a forgotten USAC dirt track mechanic as the screw jack's inventor. Whatever the case, the same basic adjustment scheme is still present in the NASCAR ranks today. One other essential component in the front suspension was a beefy anti-sway bar that in 1965 became a purpose-built through-the-frame rails unit acted on by fabricated arms.

Bringing up the rear from 1960 to 1964 was a live-axle that was suspended by parallel leaf springs and

The control cabin in Fred Lorenzen's Fairlane still mounted an OEM-style dash pad and a production-based bucket seat. The shifter and twin sidebar cage were stock FoMoCo. The strobe light mounted on the roll cage's down tube was used to check for tire wear. When the nearby lanyard was pulled and the light activated, a section of the right front tire's tread face was frozen for closer examination.

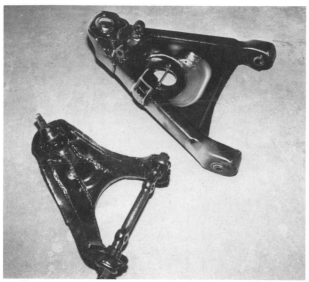

In the early fifties, few if any modifications were permitted to a Grand National stock car's suspension members. By the mid-sixties, however, teams were allowed to cut up and reweld stock suspension components, like these sixties-vintage Chevrolet A-frames, into the configuration they wanted. Totally fabricated control arms came online in the middle of the 1969 season.

housed a 9in differential and twenty-eight spline axles. After 1962, Holman and Moody used a nodular-iron center section to fill that housing, and it featured so much extra ribbing and reinforcement that differential problems were all but eliminated. In fact, that particular combination proved to be so bulletproof that it is still in use today underneath every car—regardless of make—in Winston Cup competition.

Gear selection was track specific and also influenced by things like weather conditions and the condi-

By 1963, the official NASCAR rules book permitted the use of reinforced upper and lower control arms. Fabrication skills were not what they are today, even at Holman and Moody, as can be judged by the less-than-professional-looking welds on this particular 1963 A-frame. Note the early-style weight-jacking screw and drilled front brake backing plate.

Fords—and Mopars—of the sixties rolled on rear leaf spring suspensions similar to the one used in this 1963 H & M chassis. Since screw jack adjustment of chassis preload was not possible with leaf springs—at least at first—teams added or subtracted "bite" by inserting lowering blocks of different thicknesses and by reversed "eye" or conventional main leaves. A single rear shock was used on each side, and "skinny" treaded Firestone racing tires were mounted.

tion of the racing surface. Locker carriers were generally used on short tracks and road courses during the sixties, whereas open, non-positive-traction center sections were employed for superspeedway use. Cooling was vital, especially on road courses and at short tracks where high numerical ratios generated tremendous heat. H & M's solution was to fit an Eaton power steering pump with a smaller pulley and then drive it off a matching pulley that had been pressed onto the differential yoke. High-pressure lines then plumbed the pump to an external cooler mounted on the rear floorboard just below a fan-and-shroud assembly that had been pirated from the heater plenum.

In 1965, the Galaxie line came factory equipped with coil springs and trailing arms at the rear. Holman and Moody cars, like the 1965 Fred Lorenzen Galaxie, used short, stock-style trailing arms and a specially fabricated Watts linkage—cobbled up from tie rod ends and tubular stock—to keep the new setup centered under the chassis.

After running out of Mystery Motor parts, and following a brief stint as a Mopar racer, Junior Johnson became a Ford driver in 1964. Though first driving Galaxies for Banjo Matthews, within a year he was campaigning cars of his own. That gave him the freedom to try things his own way, and in 1965 he introduced long differential trailing arms that are still in use on the Winston Cup circuit. H & M-built 1965 and 1966 Galaxies kept their third members in check by short, original equipment of manufacturer-style (OEM) trailing arms. Johnson's experience with Chevrolet coil spring cars had taught him that when it came to trailing arms, bigger was definitely better. So he began fitting the Galaxies in his stable with new front cross-members and longer-than-stock reinforced trailing arms lifted from the Chevrolet truck line. The NASCAR rules book was sufficiently vague to permit that modification, so it was allowed. Though Ford cars returned to leaf-sprung rear suspensions in 1967, the advantage in handling enjoyed by Johnson's long-trailing arm Galaxies with coil springs was not forgotten. When coil spring rear suspensions came back around in the seventies, race car fabricators—and Johnson himself, as the owner of Bobby Allison's Monte Carlo—picked up where Johnson had left off in 1966. Peek under a FoMoCo or GM Winston Cup car today, and you'll still see the same basic long-arm arrangement that Johnson engineered three decades ago.

Another rear suspension modification that began to show up when Ford cars picked up coil springs in 1965 was the addition of rear suspension screw jacks. As with the front jacks that had been in use for a number of years—and the pioneering rear jacks used on earlier coil-sprung GM cars like Smokey Yunick's 1961 and 1962 Pontiacs—the rear adjustment screws and movable spring perches were used to add or remove the grip of a particular rear tire on the racing pavement.

Chrysler Corporation was the only other factory player on the NASCAR scene after GM disbanded its racing efforts in 1963, and it had its own theories about how a race car should be built. In contrast to Ford's full-frame design, the Belvederes and Polaras that Richard Petty and Buddy Baker drove from 1962 on began life as unit-body shells that had been pulled from the line just after being "bucked." Another major difference between the early Ford and Mopar race cars was the presence of torsion bars under the beak of Grand National Plymouths and Dodges. Mayflower division and Dodge brothers cars had been using straight pieces of spring steel instead of coils since 1957, and torsion bars would continue to be a part of the racing program until the mid-seventies. In that arrangement, reinforced lower control arms carried hexagonal cups that accepted the similarly configured forward end of the torsion bars. The bars then ran to a rear-mounted cross-member, where they were held in place by two more hexagonal cups.

It was certainly a more complicated suspension system than the captured-coil spring setup used in the Ford line. It was also much more difficult to adjust to varying track conditions. Here's how Richard Petty described the process: "With the torsion bar, you had to jack it [the car] up and do all your measurements and then rewind the torsion bar and make sure the thing was in the right hexagon shape. Then you put that thing in, let it down, and wind it around. Then you had to strike it down when you put the car back on the ground and that was where it was going to go. The torsion bar had to work into the hex on each end. On the Fords, it was easier to change the suspension. You just jacked it [the car] up and changed the springs."

As with the Ford competition, Chryco torsion bar Grand National cars used reinforced upper control arms, twin shocks at each wheel, and significantly larger-than-stock sway bars. An unassisted worm-and-sector-style steering gear was also part of the program.

The handful of independent racers who continued to campaign GM cars in the sixties switched to Ford 9in third members as soon as the NASCAR rules book permitted. Smokey Yunick's 1966 Chevelles went racing with Ford differentials, for example. Chrysler racers, however, clung steadfastly to their 8 3/4in live axles during the sixties and seventies. Rules-mandated floater hubs similar to those developed by Holman and Moody were used at either end of the housing.

Ford's 9in live-axle differential quickly became a standard fixture on the NASCAR circuit during the sixties—under Ford and Brand X race cars alike. It is still in use today. This 1963 housing carries a modified Eaton power steering pump that was used to circulate axle grease between the housing and a cockpit-mounted oil cooler.

Junior Johnson is a NASCAR racing legend. His career has spanned the entire history of the sport. Many of the mechanical innovations he's added to his own cars over the years—for example, the long-style Chevy trailing arms—are now found on every Winston Cup car.

Rear axle breakage was a common problem on the NASCAR circuit until Holman and Moody developed the full-floater rear hub. That setup, developed from the Ford truck line, featured independent hubs driven by drive shafts that were splined on both ends. The hub itself rode on dual roller bearings and was retained by a sturdy large-diameter nut.

Though Ford race cars went from leaf springs to coils to leaf springs and finally back to coils during the sixties and seventies, Chryco competition cars relied on parallel leaves and twin shocks for each wheel to locate their rear end, without exception.

When Ford race cars returned to a leaf spring rear suspension in 1967, teams began to look for ways quickly to adjust suspension preload. Holman and Moody developed this setup with an adjustable rear leaf spring shackle to serve that purpose.

Holman and Moody drum brakes were developed from the Lincoln line. Drilled and reinforced backing plates were allowed by the early-sixties rules book. Fully metallic shoes and large-diameter drums were used to slow just about every Grand National stock car until Mark Donohue and Roger Penske led the sport to disc brakes in the early seventies.

Brake Wars

The brakes used to *slow*—it has been said that NASCAR cars of the sixties and seventies *slowed* rather than *stopped*—Ford and Mopar stockers were essentially identical. In keeping with the stock origin of the sport, drum brakes were mandated on Grand National cars through 1965. Even when the official rules book was amended in 1966 to allow the use of "spot or disc" brakes if they were original equipment, drum brakes continued to be the system of choice for all cars on the circuit.

Drum brake setups in the first part of the decade were essentially reinforced versions of street-going equipment, and at first, only slightly modified backing plates, shoes, drums, and wheel cylinders were used. The NASCAR rules book simply specified that "any interchangeable brake and drum assembly" could be employed. Typical race-ready changes included Swiss cheesing and scooping backing plates for cooling, and installing fully metallic linings.

By the middle of the decade, the braking system developed by Holman and Moody had become the industry standard. Based on oversized components evolved from the Lincoln line, the H & M drum brake package was built around lightweight mounting spiders that reflected the creative genius of Ralph Moody. These "backless" refinements of the original factory-style backing plate mounted a conventional wheel cylinder and a pair of 3

1/2x11in shoes that carried four welded-in-place 2x3 1/2in segments of lining. The back side of each shoe was reinforced with a network of sheet metal braces designed to resist deformation caused by extreme heat. In application, these shoes acted upon huge, finned 3 1/2x11in drums at the command of a single-cylinder master cylinder borrowed from the Ford truck line. Interestingly, most cars of the period carried no inline proportioning valves and relied solely on the stock abilities of the Ford cylinder to balance brake pressure front to rear. Power assists were not permitted. As a consequence, well-developed thigh muscles and sometimes both feet were needed to rein in a speeding Grand National car.

After reaching its final evolution in the mid-sixties, the drum brake system developed by Holman and Moody was a universal fixture on the NASCAR circuit until the road racing duo of Roger Penske and Mark Donohue persuaded the sanctioning body and its competitive counterparts that disc brakes were better. Their position was made more persuasive by Donohue's 1973 Riverside win with an AMC Matador equipped with four-wheel disc brakes. That win, scored on arguably the most demanding track for brakes on

The 11x3in drum brake setup developed by Holman and Moody quickly found its way under just about every Grand National car on pit road. At first, NASCAR required the use of stock backing plates. Later Ralph Moody developed lightweight spiders like these, to carry the fully metallic shoes that were part of the system. Reinforcement was added behind the shoes to prevent distortion under load.

Lee Petty, center, conducted Goodyear's first stock tire tests in 1958. That manufacturer formally introduced a line of special racing tires in 1958. The tire wars had be- *gun. In this 1960 shot, the senior Petty is discussing the finer points of an 8/8.2x15in Goodyear racing tire with a young son of his named Richard. Goodyear*

Firestone and Goodyear went to "war" during the sixties on the NASCAR circuit. The result was special racing rubber like these 1963-vintage Firestone Darlington 8/8.2x15in treaded racing tires.

the circuit, essentially marked the beginning of the end of the H & M drum brake system that had been in use for a decade. Gradually, all teams on the circuit made the transition to discs. As they did, a cottage industry of aftermarket suppliers sprang up to fill the need. To-

Tire failure was such a common malady during the early days of stock car racing that drivers often rigged trap doors and strobe lights adjacent to the right front tire to check on wear for themselves during a race. This is a view straight down through the floor.

day, high-tech multi-piston caliper disc brakes are standard equipment under every modern Winston Cup car.

Wheel and Tire Wars

The wheels and tires that Grand National stock cars rolled on during the sixties also went through evolutionary stages of their own. In 1960, the official rules book listed both 14in and 15in rims as acceptable, and keyed the rim width to the original manufacturer's specifications. Stock appearance was mandated. By 1966, a maximum rim width of 8.5in had been established, but 14in and 15in wheels were still legal. Rim widths increased in 1969 to 9in, and 15in wheels became mandatory. One year later, the rules book changed again, to permit the use of 9.5in rims, the same width that is used today. During most of the sixties, few Grand National cars did not roll on reinforced rims that had originally been provided by Holman and Moody. That continued to be the case even into the next decade.

Things began to change in the early seventies when the variable winds of factory support caused H & M to close down its operation. At that point, independent companies stepped in to fill the breach. One of the first aftermarket rim companies on the circuit was Norris Industries, and its slotted, stamped-steel wheels began to show up on cars like the "Coke bottle"-bodied Chargers that Richard Petty drove in 1973. Both lighter and stronger than the old reinforced "truck" rims that had gone before, the new wheels also carried five oval slots that provided the extra cooling necessary for the disc brakes that began to come into use during the mid-seventies. Modern Winston Cup stock car wheels continue to be supplied by specialty companies such as Bassett. The rules book today mandates that rims measure in at 15x9.5in. A 4.5in offset is permitted, and chrome plating is forbidden, owing to a noted tendency for plated wheels to crack under load. Modern rims still carry the cooling slots that were characteristic of the first aftermarket rims of the seventies, but more of them.

The tires that NASCAR cars have carried into battle also changed greatly during the sixties and seventies. When the Grand National series burst onto the racing scene, none of the regular production tires available in the fifties was up to the rigors of stock car competition. Blown, shredded, and just plain worn-out tires were as commonplace on the track at the typical Eisenhower-era Grand National event as beer and peanuts were in the stands.

Though the rules book permitted the use of specially manufactured racing rubber by the mid-fifties, the major tire makers of the day were slow to gear up to meet the demand. Firestone Tire Company got an early start in Grand National competition when a surplus cache of specially made sports car tires was pressed into stock car use by Smokey Yunick at the 1955 running of the Southern 500. Goodyear Tire and Rubber Company conducted its first NASCAR tire tests in 1954. One year later, Tim and Fonty Flock scored the first Grand National wins for that manufacturer while driving Chrysler 300s for Carl Kiekhaefer. Other specialty tire makers—such as the Pure Oil Company—tested the tire waters in NASCAR competition during the fifties, too. But by the time JFK moved into the Oval Office, Firestone and Goodyear were essentially the only two suppliers of racing rubber for the Grand National circuit. In 1958, the competition between the two shifted into high gear as the Goodyear-Firestone tire war began.

The earliest racing rubber molded up by those two manufacturers was not all that far removed from the compounds and designs used for everyday transport. Deeply grooved tread patterns were the norm, though Grand National stock cars never turned competitive laps in the rain. The shoulder molded into the sidewalls of early NASCAR tires was also deeply lugged like that of the tires' grocery-getting DOT brethren. Tire sizes in 1960 were determined by NASCAR's specification chart. The most common size on the circuit was 8/8.2x15in.

Tire failure continued to be a major problem, just as it had been in the fifties. Tread separations, rapid wear, and outright failure were such common occurrences that most Grand National cars of the day featured a trap door on the passenger's side floorboard, for tread inspection while the car was in motion. A lanyard ran from the spring-loaded trap door to a spot convenient to the driver. A strobe light was positioned nearby, too. When the lanyard was pulled and the strobe turned on, a section of the tread on the right front tire—the tire that carries the greatest cornering loads on the typical oval track—was "frozen" long enough for the driver to make a judgment about its further usefulness. Some stockers even carried trap doors and strobe lights adjacent to the right rear tire, too.

It was in a driver's best interest during the first part of the decade to keep close tabs on the tires. Tread or carcass failure at racing speeds usually resulted in sudden loss of control, and the consequences were often tragic. In the early sixties, Goodyear began work on a safety inner liner that was designed to keep a tire at least partially upright and inflated even if the outer part of the tread was completely shredded away. Test work was conducted by a number of drivers, most notably Darel Dieringer. It was a dangerous job, and lives were lost in the effort. Mercury driver Billy Wade lost his life, for example, while tire testing at Daytona in December of 1964, just two months after another tire test shunt had claimed the life of Jimmy Pardue at Charlotte.

The inner liner that Dieringer's daring and Goodyear's engineering staff developed was perfected in 1966 and became a rules-mandated item that same year. In practical application, it consisted of a small, treadless tire within the body of the normal racing tire. As first introduced, the inner liner seated on the inner bead of the standard 8.5in-wide reinforced rims required by the 1966 rules book. A special double valve stem permitted the separate inflation of the inner liner and the tubeless outer tire that mounted conventionally above it. Under racing conditions, if the outer tire received a puncture or simply failed altogether, the still-inflated inner liner would support the car's weight long enough for the driver to return to the pits. The number of lives saved by Goodyear's research is incalculable.

When the ever-present danger of catastrophic tire failure had been at least minimized by Goodyear's inner liner, stock car tire evolution began in earnest. In 1966, tread width was limited to 8in and "standard" tread was still required, though racing compounds were permitted. By 1969, the maximum width was expanded to a full 10in, and the rules book specified a maximum sidewall width of 12.2in plus or minus 0.15in at 60 pounds per

Perhaps the most significant technological breakthrough achieved by Goodyear engineers during their 35 years on the circuit was the perfection of the inner liner for the stock car racing tire. A tire within a tire, the inner liner keeps the tire from completely collapsing even in a catastrophic failure. Inner liners became standard equipment along pit road in 1966.

Old versus new: in the foreground is a Goodyear stock car racing Special circa 1969, and just behind it is a brand-new 1992 Goodyear stock radial.

41

Significant Car of the Period
Junior Johnson's Mysterious Impala

The year 1963 was when Chevrolet's chickens came home to roost. Five years before, GM chief Harlow Curtice had pulled off a major coup by maneuvering a gullible Robert McNamara—Ford's chief executive officer (CEO)—into accepting a supposedly industry-wide ban on all factory-sponsored racing activities. At the time, Curtice's duping of McNamara (who later became an equally perceptive Secretary of Defense under JFK and LBJ) was the most expeditious way to stop Ford's racing juggernaut dead in its tracks. Before the subterfuge that led to the AMA ban, the McCulloch-supercharged Fairlanes that Fireball Roberts, Curtis Turner, and Joe Weatherly were driving had swept the GM competition from Daytona's fabled beach course and the new superspeedway at Darlington.

With sales hurting and top mechanics like Smokey Yunick defecting to Ford's "going thing," Curtice no doubt felt he'd been pretty cagey when Ford agreed to withdraw from racing—especially when it became clear that McNamara intended to adhere strictly to the ban, even though the backdoor at Chevy's high-performance division was hanging wide open. Any feeling of self-satisfaction was short-lived, however, as Ford, not oblivious to the unstaunched flow of GM high-performance parts, decided to disavow the AMA ban and return to racing in 1960. When that happened, GM, as the ban's architect and vocal supporter,

couldn't follow suit and was, in effect, hoist on its own petard.

Still, race-minded Chevy engineers and managers did their clandestine utmost to keep "independent" racers supplied with parts and technology. Activities in these areas intensified as reactivated Ford teams—such as the Charlotte-based Holman and Moody firm—began to win races. Some of their stealthy in-house efforts, kept secret from the front office and the public alike, rival anything ever penned by spy master John le Carré. One such project was the development of Chevrolet's fabled 427 Mk IV Mystery Motor.

By the early sixties, Bill France's fledgling NASCAR was beginning to free itself from its moonshining past and gain legitimacy. The giant 2.5-mile track at Daytona had opened for business in 1959, track attendance was on an ever-increasing spiral, and the driving talents of "TV-ready" drivers like Fast Freddy Lorenzen had attracted attention from the electronic media. With Ford and Pontiac teams commanding most of the race-generated ink, Chevrolet engineers were motivated to develop an entirely new big-block engine, which would hopefully power their own "independent" drivers into the national spotlight. Building on the design of the willing, but off-the-pace, 409ci standard-bearer—of "she's real fine… " fame—they beefed up the bottom of the reciprocating assembly with a two-piece main cap system secured by four sturdy bolts. Real innovations were saved for the induction tract, however. In contrast to the

Junior Johnson drove this refrigerator white Impala on the NASCAR circuit in 1963. Though stock in appearance, it was actually quite a mystery owing to the experimental 427 MkIV Mystery Motor mounted under the hood. Unfortunate-ly for Johnson, Chevy execs got cold feet about the race-only engine and shut down production just weeks before the 1963 season. As a result, Johnson had to soldier on with just a limited number of spare parts.

409's conventional "in-line" valvetrain and shallow, almost nonexistent combustion chambers—which consisted of dished piston tops—Chevy engineers boxed up a unique set of head castings that featured canted polyangle valves and generous free-flowing passages. Small kidney-shaped "quench" combustion chambers were also incorporated into the heads—which at first, reflecting the nonproduction, race-only nature of the project, did not interchange from bank to bank. The theory behind the angled intake and exhaust valves was that distribution and flow could be improved by the unique layout. Early dyno results were encouraging, and just prior to the 1963 NASCAR season, a head-to-head comparison was arranged between Rex White's 1962 Chevrolet stocker, Junior Johnson's 1962 Super Duty Pontiac Catalina, and a new Mystery Motor-powered Impala. The test was conducted at GM's Arizona proving ground, a location chosen, no doubt, as much for secrecy as for the track located there.

Junior Johnson, a legendary stock driver and a team owner, said it took little time to recognize the superiority of the new engine design. The new Mystery Motored car was significantly faster than the previous year's cars. Johnson was so impressed with the new engine's performance that he decided to switch his allegiance to Chevrolet in 1963, and was given five of the first Mystery Motors cast to begin the racing season. A stock 1963 Impala was converted to NASCAR specs—these were the days when the word stock in stock car racing actually meant something—and plans were made for the premier event of the season at Daytona. All preparations for the Mk IV's debut were on track and quite out in the open, until just one week before the February event. Suddenly and without warning, someone in Chevrolet's hierarchy decided the Mystery Motor program was a little too exposed. Rumor has it that GM was wary of government antitrust legislation and feared that Charles F. ("Boss") Kettering's machine was about to be broken up. Whatever the case, the factory support, which had been an open secret, was suddenly cut off entirely. Corporate doges announced that the 1957 AMA ban would be followed to the letter. Exacerbating the situation for the Junior Johnson and Smokey Yunick teams—Yunick was fielding a Mystery Motored Impala for Indy driver Johnny Rutherford—was Chevrolet's attempt to "repossess" all the Mk IV engines. With just days remaining before qualifying, you can imagine the enthusiasm with which the sudden reversal was greeted around Johnson's Ronda, North Carolina, shop. After impassioned appeals, and probably a few choice words, Johnson was allowed to keep the Mystery Motors he had been given—but those would be the only powerplants he would be getting. When they were gone, no more would be forthcoming, since it had been discovered that of the forty-two Mk IVs cast before Chevrolet's loss of will, only eighteen had cylinder walls thick enough to withstand the rigors of racing.

When Ford chief Lee Iacocca's Total Performance Team got wind of the decidedly nonstock Mystery Motors that Johnson and Rutherford would be using, they vociferously protested their illegality to Bill France and company. In neither the first nor the last such decision "for the good of racing," Mr. Stock Car Racing deemed the rarer-than-hens'-teeth Mk IVs production powerplants and certified them for competition. When Ford tried to press the issue by sending John Holman to the local Chevy parts counter with the money for a production Mystery Motor, Chevrolet mysteriously—and no doubt begrudgingly—produced one, which he carted off to H & M dynos for evaluation.

Ford's worst fears about the new Chevrolet menace were realized during qualifying for the 1963 Daytona 500.

The all-new big-block 427 engine under the hood of Junior Johnson's Impala was unlike anything that had ever before come out of a GM foundry. The engine featured polyangle valve cylinder heads, free-flowing cast-iron "headers," and a unique two-piece bottom end with a four-bolt main journal. Chevrolet's famed Rat motors later evolved from the Mystery Motor.

Rutherford blistered the tri-oval at over 165mph to set a new course record. Johnson's white number 3 Impala ran just a tick slower, to start third behind Ford driver Freddy Lorenzen. Making prospects even bleaker for the Galaxie drivers were the two convincing wins Rutherford and Johnson scored in the twin 100-mile qualifying races the Thursday before the 500.

Race day dawned cold and wet, so the first ten laps of the 1963 500 were run under caution to dry the track. When the green flag fell on lap eleven, Johnson charged to the front and claimed the lead, which he held for the next twelve laps. Just as the sky seemed ready to fall on the collected Ford teams, Johnson coasted onto pit road, the victim of a failed pushrod. Rutherford lasted the race to finish ninth, but was never a factor and failed to lead a single lap. And so began a frustrating season for Johnson's Holly Farms-sponsored team. Though crew chief Ray Fox would eventually overcome the valvetrain problems that plagued the Mk IV 427s early in the season, and Johnson would go on to score six of the eight 1963 Chevrolet victories, the limited number of engines and replacement parts was never resolved. In fact, toward the end of the season when the last of Johnson's original five Mk IVs had finally expired, Johnson had to approach John Holman about buying back the Mystery Motor that Chevy had sold Holman and Moody early in the season. In a gesture of sportsmanship that also reflected the fantastic season Ford was having in 1963—twenty-three wins and the manufacturer's crown—the deal was made, and, luckily, the "Ford" Mystery Motor turned out to be one of the eighteen cast with thick cylinder walls.

When the season was through, Johnson had visited victory lane at Charlotte and Atlanta after 400-mile victories on the paved ovals there, and he'd also scored dirt track victories at Winston-Salem, North Carolina; Hickory, North Carolina; and Hillsboro, Ohio. A notable second-place finish occurred in the 1963 World 600, which Johnson led until the late stages of that grueling event, when a flat tire four laps from the flag robbed him of victory. Between seasons, Johnson readied the car for competition in 1964, but that was not to be. After deeming the Mk IV Mystery Motors legal for racing in 1963, NASCAR cavalierly reversed itself for 1964 and sent Johnson's Impala to the showers (and if you think things are any different inside NASCAR today, you

Junior Johnson wrestled his Mystery Motored Impala around the track with the help of an uncomfortable-looking stock steering wheel that had been wrapped with tape and cord. The single-sidebar cage would have offered precious little protection in a direct side impact.

haven't been to the track lately). For 1964, Johnson switched to Plymouth, then made the jump to Ford to begin an affiliation that would last through the glory years for the Total Performance Team, until 1969.

His race-ready Mystery Motor Impala sat idle in his shop for several years until he donated it to the Joe Weatherly Museum at Darlington. It was transferred from there to the International Motorsports Hall of Fame in Talladega. Museum Director Don Namon allowed us to roll the old

warrior outside for a few shots in the sunlight, perhaps the first it's seen in years. Still dressed in its 1963 racing livery, Johnson's Impala looks every bit as menacing as it must have for the Ford teams twenty-five years ago.

In strict contrast to the silhouette cars competing in Winston Cup competition today, Johnson's Impala started life as a road-going street car, a fact borne out by the surprisingly stock interior appointments, which include roll-up windows, a re-instrumented stock dash, factory door panels, and a reinforced stock bucket seat. A few changes have been made in concession to the car's racing purpose, of course. Most notable is the NASCAR roll cage, circa 1963, which looks quite spindly by today's jungle gym standards. Also, the stock steering wheel has been thickly wrapped with electrician's tape and a strand of painful-looking rope.

On the outside, the stock theme of the Impala is continued by the presence of most of its original trim and just the slightest flaring of the rear wheel openings. Save for the sponsor decals, numbers, and side exhausts, it would be easy to overlook Johnson's stocker in a Winn Dixie parking lot. Still in residence under the striped bonnet is the 427 Mk IV, which ultimately spawned a thundering herd of regular production Rat motors. Dressed in a patina of dust, in addition to its porcupine heads, cast-iron header-style exhausts, and cowl-inducted single four-barrel carburetor, the rare prototype powerplant is undoubtedly still capable of the 427hp claimed on its hood.

Though Chevrolet's Mystery Motor program was foiled by the maneuverings and vacillations of corporate management, it was still an important evolutionary engineering step on the path to the Chevrolet engines that are today dominating motor sports competition.

square inch (psi). Standard tread was still required, but by that time, tire makers were molding their racing rubber with little more than a "hen-scratch" pattern of shallow tread slots. Slicks were tried for the first time later in the 1969 season when adverse track conditions and near-200mph speeds at the brand-spanking-new super-

Today, teams along pit road marshal their inventory of racing rubber just prior to a race. Tire pressure and diameter are critical to good handling. Each of a team's tires is carefully measured prior to a race, and then assigned to a particular wheel based on its diameter.

speedway in Talladega caused tires to blister and fail at an alarming rate.

Though Goodyear and Firestone both burned midnight oil by the tanker in an attempt to build tires that could tame the new 2.66-mile high-banked track, their lack of success led most major teams to boycott the inaugural event at Talladega in September of 1969. Bill France, in an attempt to face down the newly unionized drivers who had walked out, held the race anyway—but not without scheduling mandatory caution periods every twenty-five laps so that crews could mount new rubber.

Ultimately, tire construction techniques and tread compounds were found that made it possible for the 3,900lb race cars of the era to travel safely around the circuit's superspeedways at close to the double ton. Part of that evolution involved the use of larger and larger tires. In 1971, the maximum tire width was expanded to 11in, for example, and section width grew to 12.7in at 60psi. That standard was in effect for most of the next two decades. Current rules permit even larger section widths: Winston Cup stock cars of the nineties roll on 9.5in rims, new-design Goodyear inner liners, and tires that measure up to 13.2in from sidewall to sidewall.

Firestone left the fray in 1974, bringing an end to the tire wars that had raged since the fifties. Goodyear became the sole supplier on the NASCAR circuit. Four-ply nylon Goodyear tires continued to be the exclusive choice of NASCAR drivers until Hoosier Tire Company made a foray into the NASCAR ranks in 1987. The new tire wars lasted a scant fifteen months until Hoosier withdrew from Winston Cup competition in May of 1989.

Work on an all-new radial-construction Goodyear race tire began in 1983. Sufficient work had been conducted in 1984 to permit Darrell Waltrip to conduct the first radial tire tests at North Wilkesboro, North Carolina, and that tire was admitted to NASCAR racing at the same track in April of 1989. Today, radial tires have completely replaced bias-ply racing slicks at all the events on the thirty-race NASCAR circuit.

An advantage of the new tire technology is the decreased variation in diameter that radials display from tire to tire. Bias-ply racing tires would often vary as much as an inch in outside diameter. That made chassis setup and stagger calculation demanding tasks for most teams on the circuit. Radials both vary and "grow" far less than their four-ply progenitors, further simplifying chassis setup on race day.

The new tire technology also offers several disadvantages, the foremost being greatly increased tire wear, especially at superspeedway events. Also on the down side, drivers report that the new radials have less feel than the old-style nylon tires—that is, with their far-stiffer sidewalls, they seem to provide less seat-of-the-pants feedback about their condition, and nearness to failure. A radial tire's tendency to vary less in diameter also makes it more difficult to make a quick chassis fix by simply changing tires. In days gone by, a race car with evil handling could be magically transformed into one with slot car-like grip simply by installing a set of tires with a different stagger—in other words, a different combination of outside diameters. The new crop of more uniform radials makes chassis adjustments just that—chassis adjustments. And that makes life more difficult for pit crews under racing conditions, should their initial setup prove to be wide of the mark.

Engine Wars

When corporate doges at GM pulled the plug on factory-backed stock car racing, series glory was left to Ford and Chryco to fight over. Though gone, the GM cars were not forgotten—especially the purpose-built 421 Super Duty and 427 Mk IV Mystery Motors that had powered Pontiac and Chevrolet stockers just before the corporate rug was pulled from under Smokey Yunick, Junior Johnson, Rex White, and the other GM racers on the circuit. Truth be known, the big Poncho motors were only marginally OEM at best, and not available as regular production engines at the time they first took to the high banks. Mystery Motors were even further removed from the assembly line, and never graced the engine bay of a street-going Impala.

Taking a page from the General's engine book, Chrysler engineers began working on a pseudo-stock racing engine of their own in the early sixties. Work commenced during the winter of 1962-63 shortly after the close of the NASCAR season. Chryco's big wedge motors hadn't performed up to expectations in 1962, particularly at the all-new 2.5-mile superspeedway in Daytona. Something more was needed under the hood, and Mopar engineers like Don Moore decided that it was a hemispherically chambered head casting for the raised-block engine. The target date for completing the new engine was the first part of 1964—and the annual Febru-

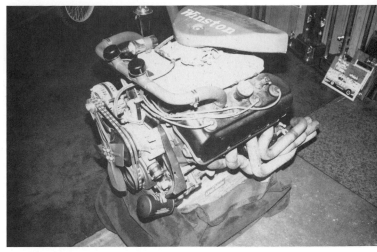

In 1964, Chrysler trumped its rivals with an all-new raised-block engine that carried heads with hemispheric combustion chambers. Though they were far from being regular production engines, NASCAR officials allowed Dodge and Plymouth drivers to field the new 426s. Richard Petty won the Daytona 500 that season and went on to his first Grand National driving championship at the helm of a Hemi-powered Belvedere. One year later, the sanctioning body reversed itself and ruled the Hemi illegal. Chryco teams boycotted most of that season, as a result.

ary running of the Daytona 500 was absolutely no coincidence. Faced with such a short deadline, Chryco engineers decided to utilize the same basic dimensions as on the 426 wedge engine in order to work with already existing tooling.

The engine they penned featured a block that had cross-bolted main journals and incorporated an additional fifth head bolt atop each cylinder bore for greatly increased sealing. A conventional cam-in-block design was employed, and the resulting pushrod-lifter combination acted on 2.25in intake and 1.94in exhaust valves that had been rotated toward the intake side of the head. Those valves were housed in fully hemispherical combustion chambers fed by a single Holley four-barrel carburetor and a high-rise-style intake manifold. When dressed out in a set of free-flowing headers and all necessary plumbing, the new engine pumped out something more than the 405hp claimed by Plymouth and Dodge drivers who trailered Hemi-powered stock cars to Daytona in 1964.

Cars equipped with the new Chrysler engine served notice of their competitiveness as soon as they rolled onto pit road. Junior Johnson recorded a lap of 170.777mph on his way to winning the first 100-mile 500 qualifier in a Hemi-powered Ray Fox Dodge, and Bobby Isaac backed that win up with another in his Ray Nichels Dodge. The coveted pole position was snared by Paul Goldsmith in a Hemi-motorvated Plymouth, and Richard Petty secured the second starting spot in his own electric blue 426 Belvedere. Ford drivers were left with a distant view of the racing pack from the minute the green flag fell. Petty took command on lap fifty-two and led the field for the balance of the 200-lap event. It

Inspired by their Chryco rivals, FoMoCo engineers started work on their very own hemi-headed engine. The new engine featured single overhead camshaft and displaced 427ci. In race-ready trim, a 427 single overhead cam motor cranked out more than 650hp. Unfortunately, *NASCAR disallowed the motor in 1966—causing a Ford-backed boycott of the circuit—and then later saddled it with so many restrictions that it never turned a single competitive lap.*

was an impressive performance—and it didn't sit well with the competition.

Shortly after the race, a hue and cry went up from Ford drivers, that the new Hemi engine was anything but a regularly available powerplant. Of course, they were right. Cars powered by the 426 Hemi were not available to the general public in 1964, and, in fact, wouldn't be for nearly two more years. Faced with the possibility of an all-Ford show following GM's withdrawal, it is obvious that NASCAR officials had decided to let Hemi cars run "for the good of racing."

Unfortunately, the folks in Ford's front offices weren't nearly so charitable. They countered the new Chryco threat with a modified version of the 427 FE engine that featured radically raised intake runners. Referred to as the High Riser, the new big-block engine produced significantly more horsepower than the Low Riser engine it replaced. By season's end, Hemi cars had won twenty-six races and the season championship. Ford drivers finished first in thirty events but were still none too happy with the new Mopar powerplant.

One other dissatisfied party was the sanctioning body itself. A Pandora's box of horsepower had been opened with the admission of the Hemi and High Riser engines, and race speeds jumped considerably during the season. When normally fearless drivers like Fred Lorenzen and Junior Johnson began to complain about

the increased velocities, NASCAR decided to slow things down a bit. On Monday, October 19, 1964, NASCAR announced a ban on both Chrysler's Hemi and Ford's High Riser. Roller cams were outlawed at the same time. One other significant change was the requirement that superspeedway cars roll on a 119in wheelbase instead of the 116in wheelbase that had been standard before.

Ford was quick to praise the new rulings—and well it might have, since Dearborn hadn't sunk the huge sums Chryco had into R & D work on the Hemi. Then, too, Ford Galaxies already rolled on a 119in-wheelbase chassis, whereas the smaller unit-body Mopar intermediates were made illegal on the big tracks by the rules change.

Faced with the loss of their promising new engine and forced to campaign Furys and Polaras at high-profile superspeedway events, Chrysler racing chief Ronnie Householder announced a factory boycott of Grand National events just ten days after the new rules were released. Ford drivers romped through most of the 1965 season as a result, and at one point won thirty-two consecutive races. The fans weren't happy with the one-marque show, however. When attendance began to lag, race promoters were quick to ask Bill France for a reprieve. It came on June 21 when NASCAR announced the renewed "legality" of the Hemi engine. Chrysler drivers returned in force in July, and won eighteen of the remaining events on the schedule.

Unfortunately for Bill France and the rest of the sanctioning body, the next broadside in the factory-backed engine war was about to be fired. When confronted with the reality of Chryco's new mammoth motor in 1964, Ford engineers had done more than cook up a new set of hogged-out head castings to sit atop their 427 blocks. In addition to developing the High Riser head package, the Total Performance Team had also set out to build a hemi-headed big-block of its own. Like the Chrysler effort, the new engine was based on existing block castings to save money. Quite unlike the 426 Mopar motors, though, Ford's hoped-for hemi featured a single overhead cam design that greatly increased the engine's ability to rev. The new design's lack of pushrods also permitted engineers to design free-flowing intake and exhaust passages, unfettered by the need to snake around the valvetrain. Timing events were set in motion by a true roller chain assembly that snaked around the front of the engine on its way from the crank to each of the camshafts in the heads. A cross-bolted block and a battleship-strength reciprocating assembly rounded out the short-block. When breathing through a single four-barrel Holley carburetor and a set of free-flowing exhaust manifolds, Ford's new hemi cranked out in excess of 600hp. Ford adherents took to calling the new 427 the Cammer, and it was on-line and ready for race duty in 1965.

NASCAR's decision to ban Chrysler's Hemi that same year had obviated the need for Ford's new engine, so no serious push was initially made to introduce it to Grand National competition. However, all of that changed, as far as Ford was concerned, when the 426 was allowed back on pit road. Ford public relations began to crank out pictures of Galaxies that had supposedly been built with single overhead cam 427s as original equipment. One such car was pictured being "delivered" to Astronaut Gordon Cooper of the Mercury 7 by racing czar Jacques Passino, for example—and Ford made it known that it planned to race the Cammer in 1966.

Well aware of the new purpose-built engine, Dodge and Plymouth engineers had an exotic double overhead cam 426 waiting in the wings just in case Ford's Cammer was allowed to run. Like the 426 it was designed to supersede, the planned double overhead cam Hemi was based on a relatively stock reciprocating assembly and block casting. The heads that bolted to that conventional long-block, on the other hand, were wildly exotic. Aluminum served as the metallurgical base for the new head castings, and each carried sixteen valves, eight individual intake runners, four siamesed exhaust ports, and twin Gilmer belt-driven overhead camshafts. Four valves for each cylinder, pent-roof combustion chambers, and a super-high-rpm rockerless twin-cam valvetrain were all pretty heady stuff for 1964, and clearly evocative of nineties engine technology. Projections called for 7000rpm operation, with 10,000rpm a decided possibility, and a power output of more than 700hp.

When NASCAR announced new engine rules for the 1966 season, Chrysler's Hemi was fully back in the fold. The 426ci versions were deemed legal for use in Mopar intermediates at all tracks of less than one mile. "Full-sized" Hemis were also available for superspeedway duty if installed in full-sized Polaras and Furys. Teams not wishing to build special cars just for big-track use

The body on Junior Johnson's Yellow Banana wasn't the only thing funny about it: the chassis was pretty unique, too. For example, the fully fabricated chassis was at odds with the "stock" chassis required by the rules book. And then there were the long-style trailing arms that Johnson had adapted from the Chevrolet truck line. Though both were outside the mandates of the official rules book in 1966, they are standard fare along pit road today.

had the option of using destroked 405ci Hemis to power their intermediates at Daytona, Atlanta, Darlington, and other high-speed ovals on the circuit.

Dodge and Plymouth drivers accepted these provisions, and things seemed on course for a renewed showdown between Mopar and FoMoCo drivers. The year 1965 had been disastrous for race promoters, owing to the Chryco boycott, and NASCAR officials were no doubt breathing a sigh of relief. If so, that exhalation of air was stopped short by Ford's December 13, 1965, announcement that it would field a fleet of Cammer-powered

When Ford boycotted the circuit in 1966, NASCAR officials and promoters alike were desperate for ways to keep the series from being a one-marque show, as it had been during the Chryco boycott the year before. As a result, Ford and Chevrolet racers were given a little extra leeway in their car-construction techniques. Junior Johnson, for example, built a special Galaxie that featured a radically pulled-down snout, a chopped and angled roof, and a radically raised rear deck. The car's odd silhouette coupled with its yellow racing livery quickly caused garage-area wags to label it the Yellow Banana. Even so, tech inspectors allowed it to run—one race. Kim Haynes Collection

In 1966, when most other Ford teams were observing a factory-sponsored boycott of Grand National racing, Bud Moore built and fielded a unit-body Comet for Driver Darel Dieringer (16). It was the first intermediate FoMoCo race car on the circuit. When the boycott ended late in the season, most other FoMoCo teams built half-chassis unit-body cars, too. The frame and suspension components developed for use in those cars are still the same basic setup used today. NASCAR Archives

Galaxies in 1966. Fred Lorenzen had lapped Daytona at more than 178mph in a single overhead cam-equipped Galaxie during test sessions that same month, and the 4mph advantage that speed represented over the race speed of 426 Hemi-powered cars was perhaps the reason Ford announced the Cammer's debut before submitting the engine for approval by the sanctioning body.

Well aware that Cammer-powered Galaxies in NASCAR competition would ultimately beget an equal number of double overhead cam Dodge and Plymouth Grand National cars, Bill France quickly took steps to block the Cammer's homologation. By 1966, the 426 Hemi engines had become an RPO in the Dodge and Plymouth lines. France made a point of visiting a Chrysler engine plant personally to inspect Hemi production. This served as the basis for a request on his part to order fifty regular production single overhead cam 427s. When Ford was forced to admit that the engines weren't really available, France announced, on December 17, that single overhead cam engines would not be permitted in a NASCAR garage area.

Ford's Leo Beebe fired back that the Cammer ban would likely make it impossible for Ford drivers to com-pete at Riverside—the season opener in those days—or Daytona, since France's December edict left too little time to re-engine the Cammer cars that had already been prepared for those events. That statement carried with it an implicit threat to boycott the rest of the season, too, if France and the sanctioning body didn't relent. France responded by modifying his stance somewhat. Ford was told that should the Cammer become an actual production engine, it would be allowed to race. Shortly after the 1966 Daytona 500, General Manager Donald N. Frey of the Ford Division claimed that a slightly detuned street version of the single overhead cam 427 had been made available to "provide smoother, safer operation on public roads." It was all fiction, of course, but France knew that Ford would most certainly walk out if Frey's announcement wasn't accepted as fact.

Desperate for some alternative, France allowed the Automobile Competition Committee of the United States (ACCUS), the US representative of the International Automobile Federation, to render the final decision on the Cammer's racing eligibility. On April 6, AC-CUS announced that the Cammer would, indeed, be al-

When the Cammer was outlawed, Ford engineers set out to "reinvent" their 427 FE motors. The peak evolution of that motor took place in 1967 when the tunnel port–head package was introduced and legalized by the sanctioning body. Though 427 Tunnel Port motors first ran with dual four-barrel carburetion, later Tunnel Ports featured single four-barrel intakes and a lone Holley four-barrel.

lowed to race—but only with a handicap. In the past, NASCAR had limited the displacement of certain engines—most notably the 426 Hemi in long-track inter-mediate-car trim. Weight had never been used to limit performance, however, and all Grand National cars in the early sixties had been required to meet a 9.36lb per cubic inch—or roughly 4,000lb—standard. In a break away from that standard, the ACCUS Cammer ruling saddled 427 single overhead cam-powered Galaxies with a requirement of 10.36lb per cubic inch—a stipulation that added nearly 500 extra pounds of power-robbing weight. Anticipating Ford's displeasure with the new weight handicap, France also took the unusual step of permitting normally configured Ford wedge-headed engines to run with two four-barrel carburetors instead of one. Three two-barrel carburetors were made legal, too.

Unfortunately, Henry Ford II was not appeased. Shortly after the rules were released, he said, "We can't be competitive under these new rules. We are giving away too much to the Chryslers. And besides that, the safety factor is quite important. We couldn't keep wheels on the car at this weight."

On April 15, Bill France's worst nightmares came true when Ford pulled all its factory-backed cars out of the scheduled North Wilkesboro race and announced it was beginning a boycott of the NASCAR circuit. For the second time in as many years, a conflict with the ever-changing official rules book had resulted in a major factory's departure from the circuit.

Though a few independents fielded Galaxies, the 1966 season quickly became every bit the one-marque show that the 1965 season had been, when Dodge and Plymouth watched things from the sidelines. Desperate for Fords in the field, NASCAR officials even permitted Junior Johnson to campaign a radically rebodied 1966 Galaxie that had received so many aerodynamic modifi-

The 427 Tunnel Port engines were aptly named. So large were their revised intake passages that the intake pushrod was forced to run through sealed tubes tunneled into the middle of each port.

Chryco engineers responded to NASCAR's Hemi ban by releasing fleets of RPO 426 Hemi–powered cars in 1966. The resulting return of Hemi-powered Dodges and Plymouths to the starting grid was galling for Ford executives anxious to have a hemi of their own. That wish was finally answered in 1969 when the all-new Boss 429 engine made its debut at the Atlanta 500. Built around an evolution of the 385 engine family first introduced in 1968, the new hemi featured alloy heads and "twisted" hemispherical combustion chambers.

Ford's Boss 429 engine was the first to carry a dry-sump oiling system. Based on components originally developed for the Ford Le Mans–winning 427 GT 40 Tunnel Port motor, the setup featured an externally driven scavenge pump, a two-piece magnesium pan, and an internally driven pressure pump.

cations that garage-area wags began to call it the *Yellow Banana*. Another novel Ford entry that showed up during the boycott was the unit-body Mercury Comet that Bud Moore had built for Darel Dieringer. Moore's decision to run with a smaller intermediate body style instead of a full-sized Galaxie turned out to be a trendsetting one. When Ford began to break ranks with the factory's boycott later in the season, many chose to return to the fray in FoMoCo intermediates of their own. By the end of September, most of Ford's big-name drivers were back in the garage area and working on 427 wedge-powered Fairlanes. Even so, the Chryco-Ford engine wars were not yet over.

One year later, NASCAR finally legalized the single overhead cam engine for competition, across the board. Surprisingly, Ford decided *not* to campaign it. Instead, Ford engineers unveiled a new wedge head for the 427 that was just as far removed from the regular production assembly line as the single overhead cam 427 had been. The castings in question featured all-new intake runners that had been relocated and enlarged greatly to enhance flow. The new ports were so large, in fact, that each intake valve's pushrod ran through a sealed tube that bisected the port just downstream from the mani-

Significant Car of the Period
Fast Freddy Lorenzen's 1965 Galaxie

Fred Lorenzen was just a fresh-faced, down-on-his-luck kid in 1961 when Ralph Moody asked him to come onboard as a Holman and Moody team driver. The amiable Illinois native had come south one year earlier, filled with high hopes, to run on the NASCAR circuit. Blown engines and failed gaskets on his independent Galaxie Starliner greatly diminished those hopes, though, and by the end of the season, Lorenzen had sold his equipment and decided to get out of racing. He was packed and leaving the track following the season finale at Atlanta when word came of Moody's job offer. That union was made official in January of 1961, and for the next seven years, Lorenzen was one of the fastest drivers on the circuit.

Lorenzen's greatest success on the NASCAR circuit came in 1963 when he became the first person to surpass the $100,000 mark in season winnings. Fast Freddy finished third in the points standings that year, won six Grand National events, and pocketed nearly $123,000. Even so, it is the refrigerator white Holman and Moody Galaxie that he drove in 1965 that ultimately had the greatest effect on NASCAR-style competition. That's because the mechanical components perfected by H & M that year and pressed into use on Lorenzen's car—and other H & M race cars—still serve as the basis for most of a modern Winston Cup car's mechanical package.

Take, for example, the chassis. Though built over a full frame, Lorenzen's 1965 mounted double-wishbone-reinforced control arms and heavy-duty spindles can still be bolted into many of the cars in the typical Winston Cup garage area. The car's front steer worm-and-sector steering box, drag link, and tie rods also quickly became industry standards that have seen constant use since their introduc-

tion nearly three decades ago. The coil springs used to keep the car's nose off the pavement were carried in spring perches that were adjusted by screw jacks, just like those on every stock car since a bit before 1965. And 1965 was also the first year that the still-in-service, H & M-style through-the-frame sway bar was installed. Twin shocks for each wheel and large-diameter drum brakes rounded out number 28's front suspension.

At the stern, a trailing arm-located 9in differential served as the basis for the other half of the Galaxie's suspension. Another pair of screw jack-adjustable coils worked in concert with four more hydraulic shocks to control jounce, and an H & M-fabricated Watts link kept the whole assembly centered around the 3,990lb car's block-long body. Two more finned Lincoln drums and fully metallic shoes completed the car's rudimentary braking system.

Power was provided by an evolution of Ford's familiar 427 wedge-headed big-block. In 1965 trim, that engine carried Medium Riser head castings that featured 2.19in intake and 1.71in exhaust valves and large, fully machined combustion chambers. A single Holley carburetor with a 1 11/16in throttle bore was fitted, as mandated by the 1965 rules book, and exhaust chores were handled by a set of free-flowing tubular exhaust headers. A wet-sump oil pan, remote oil cooler, and cowl induction air cleaner dressed out the Galaxie's engine bay. Horsepower was in the 450 to 500 range, depending on track and tune. That estimable amount of grunt was channeled back to a corporate T & C top loader four-speed and ultimately to the pavement by a set of track-specific gears mounted in a nodular "chunk." A single side carrier was used to mount those gears on superspeedways of the day, and a limited-slip center section saw duty on short tracks. The whole package rolled on a

Fred Lorenzen drove a 1965 Holman and Moody Galaxie to victory in the Daytona 500 that year. But more important than the wins scored by the car were the technological fea-

tures it incorporated, since they continued to be standard fare in NASCAR circles for the next 15 years

51

and narrower than that of stock fenders. A special header panel ran between the new stretched fenders, just ahead of the hood, to create the top of an all-new grille opening. A much-modified rear bumper was used to complete the grille surround. Cut three times, vee'd, and narrowed into an air-foil shape, the new bumper was the most labor intensive part of the whole design. A flush-fit grille was mounted just above the new brightwork and sealed tight to the bodywork with a strip of tubular rubber.

Beyond incorporating Moody's rerolled rocker panel design, the SVE staff pretty much left the rest of the new prototype's sheet metal untouched. As a result, the car didn't look all that different to the untrained eye. Even so, the new nose represented a significant breakthrough in race car aerodynamics. Total Performance Team drivers like David Pearson and LeeRoy Yarborough proved as much just as soon as the 1969 NASCAR season got under way.

Ford called the new design the Torino Talladega, after Bill France's superspeedway then under construction in Alabama. When Dodge drivers, confident of victory with their new Charger 500s, pulled into the Big D's garage area just prior to the 500, they found a fleet of far sleeker Ford aero-variants lying in wait. The cars in question had begun life as stock unit-body-construction Torinos that had been pulled from regular production assembly lines prior to the application of serial numbers or sound deadener. Delivered as bodies-in-white to the H & M "factory," the cars had first been relieved of their stock front sheet metal and frame rails, then fitted with a half chassis that had been fabricated from the front quarter of a 1965 Galaxie frame. Square-tube side rails tied the new snout into the rest of the unit body, and a full roll cage, with engine compartment loop, was used to stiffen up the cut-apart unit body.

Modified 1965 Galaxie front suspension components came next, along with a parallel leaf spring-suspended 9in third member at the stern. Lincoln drums, fully metallic shoes, and a single-reservoir truck master cylinder made up the braking system, and a pair of hydraulic shocks was used at each corner to dampen suspension oscillations. One other H & M add-on was a wrist-thick front sway bar that ran through the frame rails and carried bolt-on activating arms.

Power for the new droop-snouted Fords was slated to be that corporation's long-awaited NASCAR-legal hemi, the Boss 429. Unfortunately, an insufficient number of street-going versions of that engine had been built in advance of the 500, so each of the new Fords was forced to race with 427 Tunnel Port motorvation. Even so, LeeRoy Yarborough's Robert Yates-built Tunnel Port was more than powerful enough to beat the competition. When the checkered flag fell, it was his Junior Johnson-prepped Talladega that rolled into victory lane. Yarborough went on to win most of the major superspeedway events in 1969, in number 98 Talladegas or Cyclone Spoiler IIs (which were Mercury's version of the Talladega concept, introduced in March of 1969 along with the finally homologated Boss '9 hemi).

At the conclusion of the fifty-four-race season, not even the hurried introduction of a radically winged and beaked version of the Charger 500, called the Dodge Daytona, had been able to keep David Pearson from driving his Holman and Moody-prepped Talladega to a second consecutive NASCAR driving championship for Ford. All told, he and the other Total Performance Team Ford and Mercury drivers won thirty of the races contested in 1969.

Though originally scheduled to be a one-season body style, Talladegas were pressed into service again in 1970 after a corporate shakeup led to a withering 75 percent reduction in Ford's racing budget. Chryco had redoubled its efforts during the off-season and, in the process, had come up with an all-new winged and beaked Road Runner referred to as the Plymouth Superbird. Crippled by the lack of funding and confronting a flock of fully sponsored winged cars, Talladega and Spoiler II drivers were unable to reprise the total domination of the circuit they had enjoyed just one year before. Still, long-nosed Fords and Mercurys did visit victory lane ten more times in 1970, bringing their two-year total of wins on mile-or-more tracks to twenty-three—ten more than their much-more-aerodynamic-looking winged rivals. Radically pointed beaks and dramatically soaring wings notwithstanding, FoMoCo's Torino Talladegas and Cyclone Spoiler IIs were truly the kings of the superspeedways in 1969 and 1970.

The first Talladegas were powered by Ford's 427 Tunnel Port engine. LeeRoy Yarbrough used a Robert Yates–built 427 Tunnel Port to win the 1969 Daytona 500, for example.

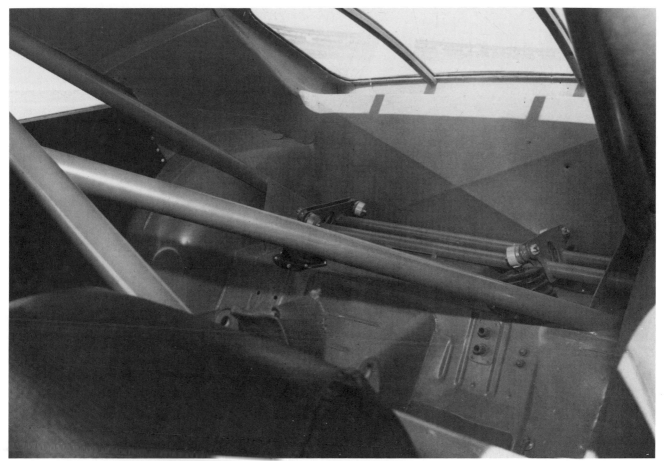

Twin shocks were used at each wheel of the Daytona. Note the still-present original backlight opening and its relationship to the flush rear window that was part of the Charger 500 and the Charger Daytona package.

426 Hemi, FoMoCo racers like Cale Yarborough, LeeRoy-Yarbrough, and David ("Silver Fox") Pearson had little trouble outdistancing Plymouth and Dodge drivers on the superspeedways. Mopar partisans knew they were in trouble as soon as Cale Yarborough put his Wood Brothers-prepped 1968 Cyclone on the pole at the Daytona 500 with a speed of 189.222mph—nearly 10mph faster than Curtis Turner's pole speed of the year before. Yarborough's performance was all the more impressive because the 427 Tunnel Port engine that had propelled him to just short of the double ton wore one carburetor fewer than the 1966 rules book had permitted on the same engine. Obviously, the only way that fewer horsepower can produce faster speeds is through superior aerodynamics, and the Torinos and Cyclones used their wind-cheating ability to the utmost in 1968. By season's end, Total Performance Team Fo-MoCo drivers had swept all the high-profile, super-speedway events, and a good many of the short-track races, too.

Dodge engineers and executives in Highland Park were less-than-pleased with their rout during the 1968 season, and even before the final half of the season were hard at work on an improved version of the new "fuse-lage"-bodied Charger. Since NASCAR rules fixed engine displacement and carburetion, they abandoned the traditional quest for increased horsepower and focused on improving the car's aerodynamics. When tests revealed that a Charger's recessed radiator opening acted like an open umbrella at speed, they moved both headlight buckets and the grille forward until they were flush with the surrounding bodywork. Aerodynamic drag was also produced by the Charger's inset backlight and the flying buttress-style C-pillars that flanked it, so these, too, were moved outward to a position flush with the rest of the body.

Dodge called the new car the Charger 500, and was so confident of its ability to beat back the Ford forces that it took the unusual step of unveiling the vehicle at the National 500 in October of 1968—three full months before its competitive debut. Among the interested parties that hovered around the car in Charlotte were Ford racing chief Jacques Passino and NASCAR coordinator Charles Grey. They might have greeted the new Dodge aero-car with concern were it not for the specially bodied Torino that Ralph Moody had been working on in a back room at the H & M complex across town.

The car in question was based on the same fast-back-style Torino body that David Pearson of H & M had already driven to sixteen victories during the 1968 season. From the A-pillars back, the car in Moody's shop was basically unchanged. It was the front of the car that had received the bulk of his attention, and the modifications he had made there were all intended to improve

David Pearson drove his blue-and-gold H & M–prepped Talladega to a second straight Grand National title in 1969. All told, Talladega and Spoiler II drivers won thirty of the fifty-four races held that season. NASCAR Archives

aerodynamics. Differences in styling between the Montego and Fairlane lines resulted in Mercury intermediate fenders that were slightly longer than their Ford counterparts. Montego fenders also angled down toward the pavement at a slightly greater angle. Moody used both of these sheet metal differences to cobble up an extended front clip that featured a stock Torino hood, Montego fenders, and a special "header panel" that ran between the two just ahead of the hood. Moody completed the new beak with a flush-mounted grille a la the Charger 500 and a new front bumper that had been laboriously fashioned from a sectioned, narrowed, and vee'd rear unit. The end result was a lengthened proboscis that presented fewer sharp angles and less frontal area to the onrushing wind than did a stock Torino's snout. One final alteration made to the prototype's unit-body was the re-rolling of both rocker panels to a position 1in higher than stock—a small modification that permitted race car fabricators legally to lower their cars a similar amount, since ride height was taken at the rockers in the late sixties.

Upon its completion, Passino and Grey took Moody's creation to Dearborn for approval by Ford chief Bunkie Knudsen. Approval was given for production, and the design was turned over to Special Vehicles Engineering (SVE) for refinement. Bill Holbrook oversaw that process, and the car he tested in the Ford wind tunnel ultimately featured purpose-built fenders that extended nearly 5in longer than stock. As with Moody's design, a special header panel connected the new stamp-

FoMoCo's entries in the factory-backed aero wars were the Torino Talladega, left, and the Cyclone Spoiler II, right. Both featured dropped snouts that cut through the air like a hot knife. They also cut through and cut up their Mopar winged car competition. During the two seasons that the aero wars lasted, FoMoCo drivers won twenty-three of the races held on tracks longer than a mile, where aerodynamics are most important. Chrysler winged cars, though apparently sleeker in design, won just thirteen mile-or-more races during the same period. Pointed beaks and towering wings notwithstanding, FoMoCo's Talladegas and Spoiler IIs were the true kings of the superspeedways in 1969 and 1970. Ford Archives

ings—welded up from shortened stock fenders and three separate new panels—and a flush-mounted grille was used to fill the radiator opening. Also similar was the much-reworked (sectioned and rechromed) rear bumper that both finished the car's new noseline and acted as a rudimentary front airfoil.

Grey had suggested to Passino that the new design be christened after the still-under-construction super-speedway in Talladega, and that name eventually stuck. When Dodge teams pulled into the Daytona garage area with their new Charger 500s just prior to the 500 in 1969, a fleet of droop-snouted Torino Talladegas was lying in wait.

Ford's original plan had been to introduce both the new Talladega body style and an at-last-legal corporate hemi-headed engine, called the Boss 429, at the race. Though a sufficient number of street-going Talladegas had rolled off the Atlanta assembly line to legalize the car in NASCAR's eyes, production of engine-homologating Boss 429 Mustangs had lagged behind. The absence of the new engine proved to be of little consequence to Ford drivers, however. David Pearson scorched the track with a lap of over 190mph to set the fastest qualifying time, and LeeRoy Yarborough went on to win the event in convincing fashion. It was the beginning of a frustrating season for Mopar drivers on the circuit.

One month later, in March, NASCAR finally permitted the Boss 429 to run, and FoMoCo marked the event by unveiling a "Talladega-ized" version of the Montego, called the Cyclone Spoiler II. The similar-but-unique body panels that were used to extend a Spoiler II's snout were actually more efficient than their Talladega counterparts. Cale Yarborough proved as much by finishing the Atlanta 500 two full laps ahead of his nearest Charger 500 competition. Ford and Mercury aero-car drivers went on to sweep just about every race but a handful of short-track events during the first half of the season.

Chrysler racing chief Robert M. Rodger was less-than-pleased by the performance of his Hemi-powered Charger 500s. Shortly after the debacle in Daytona, he and his engineering staff set out to improve on the car's aerodynamic profile. Their solution was to graft on a radically lengthened sheet metal beak that met the wind at a razor's point. When that new nose was found to produce enough down-front downforce to destabilize the car's bustle, a soaring wing was grafted to the rear quarters. This wing consisted of twin stanchions acting as vertical airfoils and an inverted wing-shaped adjustable spoiler section. The radical new configuration recorded an impressive .35 coefficient of drag (Cd) in the wind tunnel and produced 200lb of positive downforce over the front wheels. Grip was even more impressive at the rear, where each degree of wing adjustment produced 50 more pounds of downforce—up to an astonishing maximum in excess of 650lb. Winged Daytonas had so much purchase on the pavement that tire wear became a problem and tire companies had to create special compounds more capable of standing the stress.

Rodger and his crew of engineers dubbed their new winged creation the Charger Daytona and introduced it to the motoring press in April of 1969. The car's actual competition debut took place five months later at Talladega. Unfortunately, its appearance on pit road was

The year 1969 was the one in which FoMoCo finally got to campaign a hemi-headed engine of its own, called the Boss 429. The new race-bred powerplant was introduced at Atlanta in March of 1969, along with a slippery Mercury version of the Talladega called the Cyclone Spoiler II. Ford and Mercury team drivers (clockwise from upper left) Richard Petty, LeeRoy Yarbrough, Donnie Allison, David Pearson, and Cale Yarborough, pose for a publicity shot that announced the Boss '9's introduction. Ford Archives

overshadowed by a confrontation between the sanctioning body and the fledgling Professional Driver's Association (PDA) union about track conditions and tire safety. Charlie ("Chargin' Charlie") Glotzbach stunned the racing world with a (Charger Daytona) practice lap of 199.466mph—the fastest speed ever recorded by a Grand National stock car. Bobby Isaac backed up that performance with a pole-winning lap of 196.386mph during qualifying, but even so, blistered tires and complaints of rough pavement continued to be the big story in the days before the race. The PDA, led by Richard Petty, ultimately decided to boycott the race, which further muddled the Daytona's sparkling prerace performance. During the race itself, Richard Brickhouse, substituting for a boycotting Glotzbach, drove his purple number 99 Daytona to victory over a field mostly comprising Grand American (NASCAR's pony car division) Mustangs, Cougars, Camaros, and Javelins.

After Talladega, long-nosed Fords and Mercurys continued to dominate long tracks on the circuit, and not

Daytona driver Bobby Isaac won the Grand National Championship in 1970, which left both FoMoCo and Chryco one title apiece for their special aero-cars.

The interior in Bobby Isaac's number 71 Daytona was surprisingly well appointed for a race car. Carpet covered most surfaces, and the dash pad was made of vinyl. Like most superspeedway cars until 1970, Isaac's car featured full roll-up safety glass windows. Even the "wing" windows were still in place on the car.

Power to win the 1970 NASCAR Championship came from a full-race 426 Hemi. The engine in Bobby Isaac's car was dressed in a ram box, superspeedway-type intake and a sealed ram air system that connected with the cowl. A piece of foam jammed in the firewall opening served as the air cleaner in this setup.

An old-style 22gal fuel cell resided in the Daytona's trunk. Winged cars were still mostly stock unit-body stampings from the firewall back—right down to their stock trunk hinges.

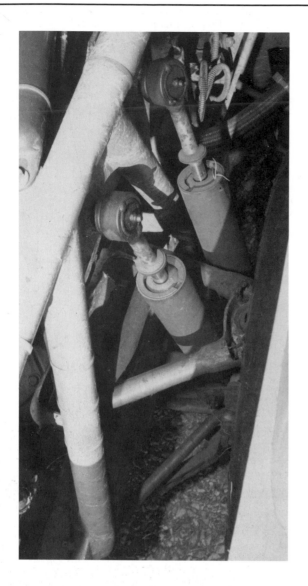

and vertical rear airfoils, he could "one-hand" his Daytona-around the track even at 200mph-plus. These sentiments were echoed by Hyde, who allowed that even the new crop of aero-Chevys and -Fords aren't as sure-footed as the Daytonas were. In fact, the spec sheet on a new T-bird shows only around 160lb of downforce produced at the rear, whereas up front, a NASCAR Ford actually has a few pounds of destabilizing lift at the near-200mph speeds it is running. Furthermore, even though Isaac's Daytona was built with a tread fully 4in wider than that on a current Winston Cup car, its coefficient of drag still would compare favorably with that of the Dodge, which is .35, and the T-bird, which is .3.

Unfortunately, after Dodge's outstanding 1970 season, the sanctioning moguls at NASCAR (as they were wont to do) decided to fiddle with the rules and place engine restrictions on aero-cars like the Daytona—effectively rendering them noncompetitive. After the K & K sat next to Hyde's Harrisburg, North Carolina, garage for nearly five years, owner Krauskopf decided to donate it to the International Motorsports Hall of Fame Museum at Talladega—and that's where it resides today.

Front suspension in Bobby Isaac's winged car was provided by a fabricated A-frame, spring steel torsion bars, and a massive anti-sway bar.

In addition to a new nose and rear airfoil, a Superbird, and a Charger Daytona, received a flush-fit rear window designed to decrease lift at the rear of the car. Stock Road Runners, and Chargers, carried recessed backlights.

until the final race of the year did one of the new Daytonas score a win on a track more than a mile long.

A number of events during the off-season would ultimately turn things around for Chrysler racers in 1970. The first of these was Ford's long-standing policy of rebodying its car lines every two years—whether they needed it or not. The year 1970 saw the introduction of an all-new Fairlane-Montego unit-body that looked even sleeker than the 1968-69 platform it succeeded. Unfortunately, looks can be deceiving—especially in the case of the 1970 Torino line. When early tests indicated that a stock-bodied Torino would be up to 10mph slower than a race-spec Talladega, work was begun on a special body aero-variant called the King Cobra.

Like the Talladega, the King Cobra was to have been relatively stock from the A-pillars rearward. From that point forward, the car was fitted with a radically reconfigured beak that looked quite like the not-yet-introduced Datsun 240 Z's. Stretched fenders and a carrier deck-sized hood were used to extend a King Cobra's—and its planned Mercury counterpart's—nose to a point farther forward and lower than stock. A ribbon-thin bumper was all that separated the hood from the gravel pan, and flush covers were used to smooth the headlight buckets that had been carved from each fenderline.

The new design looked promising on paper, and indeed the new nose created a significant amount of downforce. Things were not so rosy at the stern, however, where the stock, concave Torino backlight caused almost enough lift to pull the car's rear wheel off the pavement at racing speeds. The King Cobra design team had just about solved the lift problem with a soaring wing when an in-house shakeup at Ford sealed both the King Cobra's fate and FoMoCo's racing prospects for 1970.

The event was the dismissal of Bunkie Knudsen and the elevation of Lee ("Lido") Iacocca to the corporation's presidency. Not at all as enamored of racing as Knudsen had been, in one of his first moves as president, Iacocca slashed the corporate racing budget by a withering 75 percent across the board. The King Cobra program died an untimely death as a direct result, and the racing chances of Ford drivers on the stock car cir-

cuit went into serious decline. By 1971, Iacocca had succeeded in killing off just about every last penny of factory support for Grand National racing.

While Ford's Better Idea light bulb was dimming for 1970, Mopar racers were greeting the new season with an entirely new aero-warrior of their own. Built around a Plymouth Road Runner unit body, the new variant featured Dodge Coronet front fenders, a pointy beak similar to that of a Charger Daytona and a nearly identical rear wing. Plymouth called the car the Superbird and used it to entice Richard Petty to end his one-year stint behind the wheel of a Ford Talladega.

When qualifying was completed for the 1970 running of the Daytona 500, an aero-force of nearly twenty winged cars was ready and waiting for the handful of Ford drivers who were forced once again to campaign their 1969 Torino Talladegas and Cyclone Spoiler IIs. Though Cale Yarborough gamely put his 1969 Mercury on the pole with a qualifying speed in excess of 194mph, once the green flag fell, the race was dominated in the early stages by the winged contingent and won ultimately by newcomer Pete Hamilton in a Petty Enterprises-prepped Superbird. Drivers of Plymouth winged cars went on to win six more big-track events that year, com-

Buddy Baker became the fastest man in NASCAR history and the first to crack the double ton, in March of 1970 *when he drove this number 88 Dodge Daytona to a closed course record speed of 200.447mph at Talladega.*

Ford had advanced plans for a 1970 replacement for the Torino Talladega. Based on the newly styled Fairlane chassis introduced that year, the car was to have been called the King Cobra. It featured a radical nose that swept in a nearly unbroken arc from the pavement to the A-pillars. Unfortunately for the Total Performance Team, Lee Iacocca slashed the corporate racing budget before the season began. The end result was the untimely death of the King Cobra and a losing year for Ford on the circuit. Ford Archives

Not to be left out of the fray, Plymouth introduced a winged warrior of its own, called the Superbird. Like its Dodge counterpart, the new aero-variant featured a pointy back designed specifically to scythe through the air at triple-digit velocities.

Restrictor plates bolt in place beneath an engine's carburetor. As their name implies, they impede the flow of combustibles into the engine, and that greatly hinders horsepower production.

pared with four each for Talladega and Daytona drivers and four for Spoiler II pilots. Surprisingly, though the winged and beaked Daytonas and Superbirds appeared to be the kings of the superspeedways, the official NASCAR record book reveals that, in fact, Ford's two aero-warriors visited big-track victory lanes more often than their Mopar counterparts. During the two years that the aero-wars raged, Talladega and Spoiler II drivers had twenty-three wins on tracks 1 mile or more long, compared with just thirteen long-track wins by Superbird and Daytona drivers.

Perhaps Plymouth and Dodge drivers could have evened that tally in 1971, but an off-season rules change by the sanctioning body ruled out that possibility. Alarmed by the sharply escalated speeds the special-bodied Fords, Mercurys, and Mopars were capable of, NASCAR had first attempted to slow things down in August of 1970 by requiring all cars at the Yankee 500 in Michigan to mount a flow-reducing restrictor plate beneath their Holley carburetors. The reductions in speed produced by NASCAR's first use of the restrictor plate—

but not its last!—were evidently insufficient, because when the 1971 rules book was released a few months later, it limited the special-bodied FoMoCo and Mopar aerocars to engines of no more than 305ci. Though Dick Brooks did attempt to run a 5-liter-powered Superbird in the 1971 Daytona 500, NASCAR's new engine rule effectively brought the factory-backed aero-wars to a conclusion. Chrysler officials took the opportunity to slash their racing budget dramatically, to field just two teams. Ford and Chrysler had spent money by the tanker during the sixties in pursuit of Grand National victories on Sundays and sales floor traffic on Mondays. By the end of 1972, both of their racing programs were effectively over.

During the ten racing seasons from 1963 to 1972, the rivalry between FoMoCo- and Chryco-backed race teams had produced 177 victories for Ford, 130 for Plymouth, ninety-six for Dodge, and forty-four for Mercury. It also was the direct cause for some of the most memorable cars and engines ever to roll off an American automobile assembly line. Things would be much different in the seventies and eighties.

The roll cage used inside a Grand National stock car went through its own evolution during the fifties and sixties. Early cages were, incredibly, sometimes constructed from wood, moments before a race. Later, dual hoops and single sidebars became mandatory. In 1965, four *cage bars for the driver's side became a requirement. In 1969, when this Holman and Moody Torino Talladega was built, four bars were required on both sides of the central roll cage.*

Side glass and stock window regulators were eliminated in 1970, and NASCAR took that opportunity to require that roll cage sidebars be extended out into the empty door panel area to provide more crush space. Bar diameter and tube thickness remained constant at 1 3/4in to 1 9/10in. The year 1970 was also the one in which driver's-side window nets became compulsory. Rear diagonal bars that reached to the back bumper area came on-line in 1971, and so did an additional underdash bar and the mandatory gusseting of many roll cage intersections.

In the years since the modern era of stock car racing began in 1972, NASCAR's roll cage requirements have grown ever more stringent. Though bar size and diameter are the same as in 1960, the number, location, and gusseting of those bars has created a secure cocoon of safety for modern Winston Cup drivers, that keeps them safe from just about everything short of a direct 200mph impact. Evidence of that was provided by Darrell Waltrip's horrific, car-destroying 1990 shunt on the backstretch at the Firecracker 400 at Daytona and by Davey Allison's equally violent 1992 trip down the guardrail at Pocono. Though both accidents at first appeared life threatening, Waltrip and Allison were back

in other race cars from their competitive stables within the month. Funerals would most surely have followed both wrecks had they taken place in the same way and at the same speed in the early sixties.

Fire has long been a race car driver's greatest fear. The prospect of being trapped in a burning race car is one guaranteed to strike fear into the heart of even the most stalwart. Surprisingly, fuel cells and onboard fire systems were actually resisted by the early sanctioning body rules. Unfortunately, it took the death of Fireball Roberts to focus attention on the need for both. The tragedy took place at the 1964 running of the World 600 in Charlotte. An early race altercation between Junior Johnson and Ned Jarrett drew Roberts' Passino Purple Holman and Moody Galaxie into a multi-car wreck that ruptured his fuel tank and started an inferno that inflicted severe burns over most of his body. Roberts succumbed to those injuries three months later.

By the beginning of the 1965 season, rubber companies were hard at work on a fuel cell that would be acceptable to the sanctioning body. In 1967, the official rules book was amended to require the use of an approved 22gal fuel cell in all Grand National cars. Much the same requirement continues today, and steel canis-

Significant Car of the Period
Smokey Yunick's Secret Weapon

Henry ("Smokey") Yunick has always been what you might call a freethinker—especially when it comes to things mechanical. Since his earliest days as a Penn State racer of incontinent British motorcycles—hence his nickname—Yunick has been interested in making mechanical things run faster. Following his discharge from Army Air Corps service in World War II, Yunick moved to Daytona Beach and set up his self-titled Best Damn Garage in Town. The World's Most Famous Beach was a hotbed of racing activity in the forties and fifties, and soon Yunick was a regular fixture on the NASCAR circuit. The Hudson Hornets he built for Herb Thomas led to Grand National driving championships in 1951 and 1953. When General Motors introduced its all-new small-block engine in 1955, Yunick was one of the first race car builders to put it to the test. He and Thomas teamed up to announce that engine's arrival by winning the 1955 running of the Southern 500 at Darlington. Later, when wide-track Pontiacs showed more promise than other "stock cars" of the day, Yunick became the first car builder to win back-to-back Daytona 500s when Marvin Panch (1961) and Glenn Roberts (1962) put Yunick's trademark black-and-gold cars in victory lane.

Much of Yunick's racing success is directly attributable to his ability to devise new ways to make a car perform. Unfortunately for NASCAR rules book writers, Yunick's interpretation of the official regulations governing the fledgling sport was often at odds with their views. In Yunick's opinion, if the rules book didn't specifically forbid a particular part or practice, then it must be legal. Take, for example, the fifties-era ban on port modifications that left telltale machining marks. Yunick rigged up a slurry of sand and water that

When NASCAR officials balked at the bodywork on Smokey Yunick's first 1966 Chevelle, he built this template to prove the car was stock. It was one of the first such devices used in NASCAR. Tech inspectors ultimately let his allegedly 15/16-scale Chevrolet run.

when drawn through a head casting, ported it just as effectively as the best die grinder—without leaving any traces. Or how about the Anaconda-sized fuel lines he fitted to his cars when NASCAR officials began limiting the size of a car's gas tank. Yunick's bag of tricks also included moving a race car's body around on the frame rails to improve handling, which technically didn't violate the rule that prohibited moving an engine's location for the same purpose.

Reverse-rotating engines that better loaded an oval track car's chassis, hidden oil reservoirs, smoother frame

Few cars have received as much print, or inspired as many stories, as the Chevelles Smokey Yunick built in the mid-sixties. Though Yunick's black-and-gold Chevrolets were built in the gray area of the NASCAR rules book, they prob-ably weren't as illegal as some legends contend. Then again, maybe they were. Does the body of this particular Yunick Chevelle seem a bit pushed back on the frame to you?

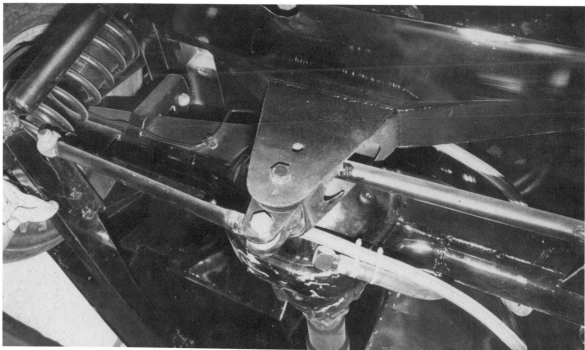

The underside of Smokey Yunick's Chevelle was an engineering marvel. The car rode on a fully fabricated frame that featured offset front and rear snouts to bias the car's weight to the left, for better handling in the corners. Custom-made trailing arms were used, and so was a belly pan. Yunick even made the lower Watts link arm into a teardrop shape for better undercar airflow.

The 1967 NASCAR rules book said you couldn't move an engine's position relative to the frame to change weight distribution. It did not say you couldn't move the whole frame, however. So that's just what Smokey Yunick did with the destroked 427 he installed in the car. He also used the engine's block as a stressed member of the frame.

members for better aerodynamic flow, hydraulically adjusted suspensions, mushroom lifters, nitrous oxide, and a host of other modifications were all part of Yunick's bag of tricks at one time or another in the fifties and sixties. The challenge of circumventing the rules and beating his on-track rivals—who were, no doubt, doing a little interpreting of their own—was obviously the primary attraction Yunick felt for racing during NASCAR's first two decades.

As may well be expected, NASCAR officials took a dim view of Yunick's ingenuity. The clashes Yunick had with Big Bill France as a result became the stuff of legends around a NASCAR garage area. The Chevelles Yunick built from 1966–1968 were the focus of more than a little controversy during their time on the track. Though ultimately none of the cars that were built ever visited victory lane, they still collectively rank as some of the most innovative and significant cars ever to grace a Grand National pit road.

Yunick's Chevelles first attracted attention at the 1966 Dixie 500, when competitors charged they were less than full-sized. Those rumors intensified when Curtis Turner and Yunick showed up with a Chevelle at the 1967 Daytona 500.

Both waited until the last day of qualifying during Speedweeks 1967 to make an appearance in Daytona's garage area. Minutes before the track closed for the day, Yunick unloaded the car, and Turner took it out on the track. Three laps later, he had shattered the record books with a 2.5-mile trip around the banked oval at 180.831mph.

After Turner idled back to the garage area, Yunick pulled a car cover over the Chevelle, and both men left the track—leaving the rest of the teams on hand to scratch their heads. During the race, though an ill-timed fuel stop put Turner one lap down, he was able to make up that deficit in just five circuits of the track. He seemed destined to overtake and pass eventual race winner Mario Andretti, driving a Holman and Moody-prepared Fairlane, until the 404ci 427 that Yunick had built (another of his tricks) expired.

The 1967 Atlanta 500 was the next stop on the circuit for Yunick and his Chevelle, and NASCAR officials were waiting for both. The upstart Chevelle's Daytona performance had caught the attention of competitors and rival car manufacturers alike. They concluded that the only way a non-factory-backed independent race car could run so well was to cheat, and rumors had been flying about the car almost since the moment of its February debut. A significant number of those tales focused on the Chevelle's diminutive size. Before long, stories were circulating that the car had actually been built to 15/16 scale—and that's what NASCAR tech inspectors accused Yunick of at Atlanta. To answer their questions, Yunick produced a template he'd made of the car's body—possibly the first template ever seen in a NASCAR garage area. Yunick dispatched a crew member and a NASCAR official to rent a stock Chevelle from Avis, and then compared it and Yunick's black-and-gold number 13 race car against the template. Both fit. In-

Smokey Yunick was always a safety advocate on the circuit—and that's why he installed so many extra bars in his Chevelle's roll cage. Their addition to rigidity and handling was just a bonus. The location of the car's bucket seat, low and to the extreme left, was not an accident; it was one more attempt to move the car's center of gravity to enhance handling in the corners.

Smokey Yunick moved as many components in his Chevelle as far left as he could in search of better weight distribution—like, for example, the decidedly off-center fuel cell.

terestingly, when the same template was fitted to another "legal" Chevelle in the garage area, it was off by a mile. NASCAR officials backed down, and Turner was allowed to qualify, but the legend of Smokey's 15/16-scale Chevelle was born. Unfortunately, Turner destroyed the car in practice. When Chevrolet, nervous about all the publicity the Chevelle had been creating, asked Yunick to return any corporate R & D pieces on the car, Yunick had the car crushed into a cube and sent to Detroit.

For 1968, Yunick built another 1966 Chevelle to run in the Daytona 500, this one to be driven by Indy star Gordon Johncock. The new car represented all that Yunick had learned about making a race car perform. Its design included features that, though radical—and even illegal—by 1968 standards, are commonplace in any NASCAR garage today.

Since just about every car builder of the day was using Ford parts and even Ford frames under his or her race car, Yunick interpreted that to mean he could build his own frame in-house: if other cars weren't stock, why should his be? It was a visionary and pioneering step that today is being taken by teams like the Goodwrench-Richard Childress-Dale Earnhardt combination that has done so well in the nineties. Yunick's decision allowed him to try things he'd been considering for a number of years—like, for example, mounting the floor pan flush with the bottom of the frame's side rails. Though the NASCAR rules book permitted belly pans, it was mum about where to mount a race car's floor pan. Mount it low enough and, voila! instant belly pan. To add to the effect, Yunick moved every undercar component he could, including the exhaust system, up inside the floorboards. The components he couldn't relocate—like the lower Watts link bar—he tear drop-shaped to decrease wind resistance.

To complement the new belly pan, Yunick split the stock front bumper and then added a couple extra inches of metal before having it rechromed. The result was a pretty effective—if highly illegal—front airfoil. A flat section of metal was mounted just behind the bumper, and it directed undercar air to an extra-wide wet-sump-style T-shaped oil pan that was the third element in Yunick's air management plan.

On big left-turn ovals like Daytona, it is optimal to put as much weight as possible to the left of a race car's chassis. That way, centrifugal force will tend to even out chassis loads in the corners. NASCAR officials were well aware of this fact and had written many rules to keep teams in check. The most important of those was a ban on moving

the engine from its original location between the frame rails. Tech inspectors checked for alterations of this type by measuring to see that the engine was centered in the rails. But they never measured to see if the rails themselves had been moved. So that's exactly what Yunick did: build his frame with offset snouts, front and rear. While re-engineering the chassis in his Chevelle, he also made its 427 block a stressed member of the frame for greater torsional rigidity and better handling.

Yunick also made sure to bias Johncock's seat as far as possible to the left. To do that required building the left side of the car from the inside out—roll cage first, window and regulator next, and then outside door skin. Finally, he biased the car's trunk-mounted Firestone fuel cell—another Yunick innovation that NASCAR officials had, incredibly, been reluctant to allow—to the left, too.

The suspension Yunick cooked up for his 1968-season 1966 Chevelle was every bit as trick as the frame it bolted to. Owing to problems with stock components the year before, Yunick built his own fabricated control arms—in another move that anticipated rules book changes several years distant—and made cambers adjustable by integral turn buckles and Heim joints. A revised front steer setup was employed to provide an optimal Ackerman angle and to make room for the 427's belly pan-style oil pan.

The car's rear suspension consisted of a Ford 9in third member, fabricated trailing arms, and coil springs that were assisted by Air Lift bags and mounted behind the axle's tubes. A custom-made Watts link kept everything centered under the chassis. A differential cooler was mounted inside the trunk and vented through a small screen in the rear pan.

Power for the 3,900lb package was provided by a destroked version of the Chevrolet Rat motor that displaced 416ci. Yunick's theory was that less reciprocating mass meant higher backstretch rpm and decreased fatigue. His 427 with its 3.56in stroke by 4.312in bore was good for 7600rpm and produced more than 450hp. Those ponies were fed by a ram air induction system that funneled air from the Chevelle's windshield area through the cowl to a sealed twin-scooped air cleaner. Since each 10-degree-Fahrenheit drop in mixture temperature equals a 1 percent increase in power, Yunick clothed the whole induction system in heat-resistant thermal wrap.

All the one-off hardware Yunick had built into his Chevelle was housed in a sheet metal package that contained a few tricks of its own. Aft of the "non-stock" bumper, all the car's rough edges were smoothed to reduce wind resistance. This included fitting the wheelwells with close-fitting inner fenders that were smooth as a baby's bottom, making sure the bumpers fit within the car's side bodylines, and fitting the roof with a subtle "vortex"-generating dip that directed air to the diminutive deck lid spoiler that the rules book permitted.

Word of Yunick's new Chevelle preceded him to the track in 1968, and NASCAR inspectors were lying in wait with a list of revisions he'd have to make in order to race. First and foremost of these was the stipulation that he remove the car's frame and replace it with a stock unit. Less than pleased with NASCAR's response to his handiwork, Yunick threw a couple of gallons in the car's fuel tank and drove the car home from the track in afternoon traffic. The next day, the headlines read that he had driven the car back to the shop without its fuel tank—which was perhaps true, since he'd left the cell's steel liner in the pit area—and another Yunick legend was created.

Yunick recently completed a restoration of his old Chevelle, and today it belongs to collector Floyd Garrett.

Modern-day drivers have a better chance of surviving a serious shunt owing to the roll cage rules that have evolved with the sport. Darrell Waltrip's wild ride in the 1990 Firecracker 400 destroyed his Lumina but only bruised his ego. A modern roll cage is seen here along with Waltrip's Lumina.

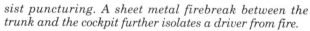

Firestone helped develop the 22gal fuel cell that today is an integral part of every Winston Cup car's trunk. The cell is housed in a metal box that itself is designed to re- *sist puncturing. A sheet metal firebreak between the trunk and the cockpit further isolates a driver from fire.*

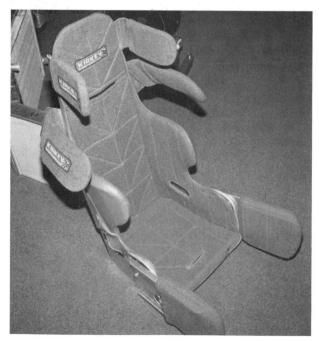

Today, ergonomically correct custom-made seats are used that offer the utmost in comfort and safety.

ter-mounted 22gal fuel cells are still mandatory equipment on every modern Winston Cup stock car.

The onboard fire-extinguishing systems that are now mandatory in a NASCAR race car evolved in much the same way. Early-sixties stockers usually had no firefighting gear onboard. In fact, it wasn't uncommon for drivers to spend 5 hours at speed behind the wheel, dressed in their normal street clothes and wearing only a rudimentary helmet. Legendary Curtis Turner once drove a race in a tuxedo when a car owner complained about his messy driving suit, for example. Later in the decade, Holman and Moody developed a remote-discharge fire bottle system that was activated by a single lever located close to the driver's right hand. By the end of the decade, more sophisticated systems came on-line and Nomex driving suits along with high-quality safety helmets had become high fashion along pit road. Today, the official rules book mandates a high-pressure Halon fire system that has outlet ports under the hood and in the trunk as well as in the driving compartment. As a result, though fire continues to be a fear for drivers on the circuit, it is much less a threat than in Fireball Roberts' driving days.

Driving seats are another often overlooked area of safety. In Strictly Stock and early Grand National days, stock, unmodified seats were mandated. Since most cars of the era came equipped with benches, that meant drivers had precious little restraint in an accident. "Factory-manufactured" seats were still required by the rules book well into the sixties. Buckets were allowed, and so was extra reinforcement designed to help keep a driver in place behind the wheel of a car. Lightweight van seats were the norm, and fabricators often augmented them with rudimentary side bolsters made from sheet aluminum. Though better than the bench seats that had gone before, sixties- and seventies-vintage racing seats were still but little removed from the showroom floor.

Aluminum-bodied buckets came on-line during the late seventies and early eighties when NASCAR's continuing requirement for a manufacturing origin was reinterpreted to include aftermarket specialty seats. That requirement was loosely enforced, however, and many of the less-well-financed teams continued using van seats or began to build their own out of sheet stock or other material. One early Bill Elliott car was discovered, during a recent restoration, to have a seat welded up from Dawsonville, Georgia, road signs, for example.

The seats drivers ride into battle today are custom-fitted affairs that have been carefully fabricated from aluminum panels. The modern rules book requires padded rib protectors, padded leg-protecting extensions, and a NASCAR-approved headrest. These provide the maximum in driver safety and protection, and consequently cost hundreds of dollars each to build. But the near-200mph velocities common on the circuit demand nothing less.

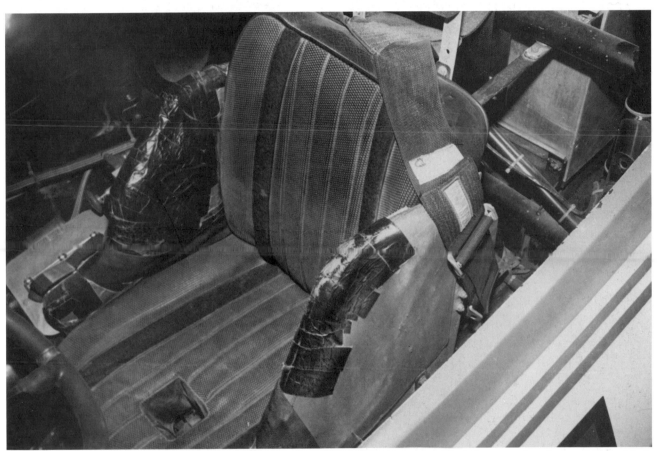

The shape and size of a stock car's seat have changed greatly over the years. Originally, unmodified bench seats were required. In the sixties, "production-based" buckets were required, but extra bracing could be added to keep a driver in place.

Wayne Torrence: Veteran of the Tire Wars

Wayne Torrence has been around NASCAR racing for a long time—more than thirty years, in fact. Most of that time has been spent as the manager of Goodyear's racing tire warehouse in Charlotte. In that capacity, he's had a first-hand look at the evolution of the stock car racing tire. I asked him to trace those steps for us.

A.—The company was in racing in the early part of the 1900s, I'm not sure when, and then got away from racing. If I'm correct, they started testing "stock car tires" probably about 1964 on the NASCAR convertible series. Then in 1965, they were actually racing in that series. Then in 1966, we actually started a big-league first down in Darlington, on what used to be called the Grand National. I guess it was in 1967 when we actually started participating in the Grand National series. That's when the so-called tire wars started that lasted into the seventies. They were all basically four-ply bias-construction tires. In the early stages, we did have a trim tire. A tire that some call slicks. So you don't have a tread design. I'm not sure exactly what stage it was when we went from a treaded tire to a slick.

Q.—In the seventies?

A.—Late seventies or early eighties was when that change was made. But really, that wasn't a major development. Back then, we made a lot of changes in constructions to continually try to improve the tire. Then in 1986, we started working on a radial stock car tire. We actually ran radials in 1987 and '88. First race in Winston Cup was in 1989. We had just this year completed the entire circuit.

Q.—It is all radials now?

A.—The fall '92 race at Bristol will be [was] the last race we race on bias-ply tires.

Q.—Will you stop making the bias-ply tires?

A.—We make them for use on short tracks and weekly short tracks. As far as Winston Cup racing goes, we'll surely cut back.

Q.—Do you have different radial compounds for different tracks, or is the same tire used everywhere?

A.—No, there are different compounds.

Q.—Is basic tire construction the same for all radial tires?

Wayne Torrence

A.—Actually, we have, in essence, more than two constructions on the radials: the superspeedway tire and the short-track tire.

Q.—How do they differ?

A.—The superspeedway tires are taller. They are run 88in on [the] right and 87in on the left. On a short track, we use 87in on the right and 86in on the left. The degree of stagger varies from track to track. Other than NASCAR's rules and regulations, you can only have an inch in stagger. That will probably be changed in the near future. But that rule was written in the bias days to prevent too much stagger. They only allowed an inch. You could probably get it up to 2in to 2.5in with air pressure. You can't do that with a banded tire. You can't expand a radial.

Q.—Do you mold and band at specific diameters?

A.—Yes.

Q.—So you have an 88in mold and an 87in and an 86in ?

A.—Well, 86.5in, 86.75in—anywhere from 0.375in stagger to 1in stagger at this particular time.

Q.—Is that intentional, or is that just a result of molding?

A.—That is design. We may run 0.375in stagger at a given track, or we may run an inch. At Michigan, we ran an inch of stagger. At Atlanta, we ran radials down there the spring race, and quite obviously we had some problems, and there were a lot of them. We proceeded very slowly with the radial. Actually, we have made a lot of improvements in the tires. The cars are definitely much improved. [They have] Better suspension.

Q.—In addition to height, what other core differences are there? How does the stickiness of the rubber vary?

A.—We can't really get into discussing that area. For the layperson, the construction of the superspeedway and the short-track are really the same.

Q.—The height is the major difference?

A.—Right.

Q.—How would you describe the difference in compounds to a layperson?

A.—It is the hardness of the rubber compound that is used. We use a softer compound on the shorter tracks. At Martinsville, we use the softest compound we run anywhere in Winston Cup because the track is so flat and not very demanding. We use the hardest compound at Daytona and Talladega—high-speed and high-banked tracks. There is a range of compounds for short tracks.

Q.—It is now possible to run a whole race on a set of tires?

A.—At Talladega, they probably could have. Some Busch cars did run 300 miles on the tires. There are some tracks, Daytona and Talladega among them, where new tires aren't going to help. On some of the other tracks, they make all kinds of difference. It is the surface—a combination of a lot of things.

Q.—Racers used to "scuff" bias-ply tires to make the car handle better. Is that still necessary with radials?

A.—It is not necessary with radials. People scuffed the bias-ply tires because, being bias-ply, they were going to grow. In a radial, the size is not going to change.

Q.—How much growth is there?

A.—There is none.

Q.—None at all? So, if it is molded at 88.25in, it is going to be 88.25in at the race?

A.—You can hardly change the dimensions of a radial tire with air pressure. What you do change with air pressure in a radial tire is its spring rate. It is like putting in stiffer springs.

Q.—So it affects the sidewall more than the tread?

A.—Yes. It is probably 50/50 now.

Q.—How do radials and ply tires compare in puncture resistance?

A.—The radial is much more puncture resistant. That was one of the areas we wanted to work on—especially for races like Pocono, it was bad, and Sears Point, [where] it was extremely bad.

Q.—How about the inner liner? Wasn't Goodyear responsible for that innovation?

A.—Yes.

Q.—Did Darel Dieringer do a lot of the tire testing?

A.—Darel was a basic tester for us. He helped. You probably know that later he went to work for us. He did the testing on the inner liner, and we basically used pretty much the same inner liner all these years, up until last year when we brought out the tubes.

Q.—How did the new liners differ from the old ones?

A.—They don't use the tube.

Q.—And before? There was a tube?

A.—Before there was a lifeguard safety spare, which in essence was a four-ply tire without any tread. We could inflate and adjust the pressure in both of them [the inner liner and the outer tire] with one valve. You were in essence running tubeless. The tire was running all the time 20 to 25lb more of air pressure than the liner. There was always at least a 20lb spread.

Q.—So, for example, the outer tire would be 60psi and the inner tire would be 90psi?

A.—That's so that you wouldn't collapse the liner from the outer pressure. Some tracks—Daytona and Talladega—there is a 25lb spread. Three or four years ago, we got out of the tube business. Now we go to the outside to have our tubes made. We haven't increased the number of equalizations.

Q.—Can you explain what that means, when they say the tire pressure equalizes?

A.—Let's say you are running 50lb on the right side, and the inner tire is 70lb of pressure. If something happens, then pressure goes to 60/60. The air is going to equalize between the two chambers. Remember, the shield of the spare weighs about 10lb. The tube weighs about 4lb. As a result, you have roughly 14lb of dead weight in there flopping around. That sets up a tremendous vibration. We were experiencing more and more problems with that. So we worked real hard on the development of a tubeless shield. We now have two valve stems in the wheel, and they are inflated or deflated separately. The principle is the same except the shield itself sits on the wheel just like the tire does.

Q.—Does that mean that they had to make a special wheel?

A.—No. They were able to drill the existing wheels. It takes a special valve. We use a regular "short straight" valve in the standard opening in the wheel, and then there was a special-designed valve that was flush on the inside. The second valve is for shield inflation. It has worked extremely well. We have had very few equalizations. Most of them are due to a stem failure. We hope if it does equalize now, it doesn't set up a vibration. In fact, drivers probably won't know it because they run on more air pressure. I discovered that in Ohio in testing. When the drivers came in and we were testing the tube or shield that day and we checked the left-side tires, everything was fine. Then we purposely equalized the right front. We told the driver we were trying something, and if he felt anything at all, to get out of it and come back. He ran ten laps with the right front equalized. He didn't know it. That was a plus.

Q.—The inner liner is designed to do exactly what?

A.—It is just another tire inside the outer tire, that you

A modern Goodyear radial (right) is both wider and taller than the 8/8.2x15in Blue Streak racing tires used in previous years. Note the vestigial tread pattern on the late-sixties tire on the left.

can continue running on to get back into the pits.

Q.—It would be good for a lap at speed, or something like that?

A.—Yes—if the outer tire was like a radial tire. When radials run very seriously underinflated, that throws the tread package off. If that happens, you are going to have to get in pretty quickly because you are running on the inner liner itself, which is a four-ply tire, in essence. But it doesn't have any tread on it. Just enough rubber for it to stay together. At Talladega you would be lucky to make a lap. Short track, maybe you could make a couple, but it would eventually wear through that.

Q.—You've said the radials have outstanding wear compared to the old tires. Can you compare, for example, in 1989 at Talladega, the number of tire changes a team would have to make to get through that 500-mile race compared to today.

A.—At Talladega, [you needed] ten sets of [bias-ply] tires. Because the actual big plus on the radial is being able to control and maintain the size and know where they are all the time. You could work on the car with that. When under a bias-ply, you never knew where you were. You had to take them off and measure them. You knew what you put on, and that was particularly bad if you only had to change two tires.

Q.—In the old days, drivers actually checked tires during a race, with a strobe light. Was that for wear?

A.—It was for wear and also to be sure the tire wasn't blistering. Back in the tire wars days, that was fairly common. You had to run on the edge to be competitive.

Q.—What does that mean? Why were the tires more inclined to blister? Were you making them out of a stickier compound at that time?

A.—A stickier compound, which is basically plastic.

Q.—But it didn't last nearly as long.

A.—No.

Q.—Why did you go to slicks? Was that a rules-mandated change, or was that an evolution for performance?

A.—No, it was just an evolution for performance. The only purpose for tread is to release water.

Q.—Did NASCAR make you keep the tread on during the fifties and sixties?

A.—That was something we did ourselves. NASCAR only says the four tires must be alike.

Ralph Moody: Truly Legendary

The term legendary is often misused, especially in the realm of motor sports. Today's hot driver or team manager is often tomorrow's unknown, no matter how many times the word legendary is applied during his or her streak of success.

Still, some personalities in racing have truly become legends in their own time, and Ralph Moody is squarely in their number. Though most recall him as one-half of Ford's Holman and Moody racing factory, Moody's days on the circuit actually began years before he ever met John Holman. In fact, at one time, Moody was one of the hottest drivers in the stock car ranks. He had made a name for himself in the early fifties driving the northeastern bullrings. In 1956, Pete De Paolo signed up the Massachusetts native to drive one of his factory-backed Fords. It didn't take long for Moody's name to start showing up in the top ten, and in June of that year, he won his first Grand National race, in LeHi, Arkansas. He went on to win three more races that season, and finished eighth in the points with his number 12 Ford.

His ride with De Paolo introduced him to Holman, who had been hired to run the East Coast arm of De Paolo's Long Beach-based operation. One season later, when Ford and De Paolo parted company, Holman and Moody was born. With Holman in charge of business affairs, Moody put his mechanical skills to work building winning race cars. When Ford abruptly abandoned all forms of factory-backed

Ralph Moody

motor sports in 1957, Moody and Holman soldiered on as an independent concern. In 1958, Moody supervised the construction of a fleet of turnkey Thunderbird race cars that were available to anyone with the necessary cash. It was a concept that was years ahead of its time. More customer Fords were built in subsequent seasons, and when Ford officials decided to return to racing, Holman and Moody was the logical choice to supervise that venture.

The sixties were golden for Ralph Moody, John Holman, and their H & M racing "factory." With factory money flowing like water between Dearborn and Charlotte, H & M built everything from AF/X drag race Mustangs to Grand National stock cars. Drivers like Fred Lorenzen, Fireball Roberts, Curtis Turner, Cale Yarborough, Dick Hutcherson, David Pearson, and Bobby Allison were hired to drive the Galaxies and Fairlanes that Moody built, and racing victories followed in short order.

Many of the racing components that Moody developed and perfected became standard equipment on race cars of all stripes in the sixties and seventies, and H & M-evolved components are still in use on the circuit today. Reinforced stamped-steel wheels, heavy-duty hubs, fully metallic drum brakes, component sway bars, Galaxie-based steering systems, onboard fire systems, adjustable spring perches, and a host of other components that were needed to go stock car racing in the sixties and seventies were all either invented or perfected by Moody and the H & M crew.

As if becoming the dominant force in Grand National racing wasn't challenge enough, the sixties also saw H & M help develop Ford's Le Mans-winning GT 40 endurance car and an assortment of other Ford-derived sports cars. H & M opened a Ford-based high-performance marine shop in Miami, Florida, during the same period.

Unfortunately, a corporate leadership change in 1970 stanched the flow of factory dollars that sustained H & M through the sixties, and by 1972, H & M was no more. It's likely that no one organization will ever dominate American motorsports as completely as Holman and Moody did during the sixties.

Today, Ralph Moody lives in semi-retirement in Charlotte, not far from the mostly vacant H & M airport facility.

Q.—What can you tell us about your heydays with Ford in the sixties? How fully did the corporation back Holman and Moody? How much work did you perform in-house?

A.—Holman and Moody was fully backed. Whatever it took, that's what they did. We were Ford racing at that time. All the racing was handled out of the Charlotte shop. If you wanted a piece or a performance part, that's where you got it. We had a complete line to do all the head and block work on a 427, 429s, and all that. We did the complete work on all that stuff. It came in raw castings, and it was all done there. We made all the cranks, steel billet stuff. All that kind of stuff for boats, street cars, and race cars. Made all the sway bars. All the things you can think of, we made there. Even the spindles came rough. We made our own axles, our own sway bars. All the scrunched stuff would come in billet forms, casting forms, and we would do all the finish work there. It was all automatic and that kind of stuff. All the marine stuff was done the same way. A lot of it came out of Atlanta. A lot of casting came out of California.

Q.—How many were in your work force at the time?

A.—Probably, between Miami, California, and Charlotte—450 people.

Q.—Who was the toughest driver who worked for you?

A.—I guess Cale [Yarborough] might have been, but he didn't stay with us long. He was about as hard as anything, 'cause he would just over drive it and get into the wall when he first started. David Pearson was really easy on a car. [Fred] Lorenzen was not hard on a car. They were pretty knowledgeable about how much a car would stand. They were in a position where they could get along with themselves and everybody else, 'til near the end of the race, and then they would go for the win. Today, you'll find the big ones will sit back until the end of the race. Pretty much today, it is the same as it was back then. You just pretty much have to control your driver from the pits and tell him what you need, where he ought to be, and what he is doing and where he is running.

Q.—Tell us about Fireball.

A.—He used to live with me. He was a problem sometimes. When I first knew Fireball, he drove modifieds. I knew him in Florida. That was back before we were thinking about Holman and Moody, and, boy, he was really getting irritated. We used to give him a pretty hard time about the cars I had. Of course, then I got to know him in Grand National, which is Winston Cup now. Fireball was a heck of a short-track racer, but [with] some things he just had to catch up. He just hadn't been there yet. He and I got along pretty good. We used to go to places and help him with the problems he had. He couldn't run a place like Martinsville because he just didn't have the knack to know what to do with it. But after we got him there and got him to understand what I was doing, then he got pretty good at that type of racing. He would wear the tires off the car. He used to wear the brakes out. He used to run modifieds, and he didn't have to worry about things like that. It didn't take him long to pick it up. But he was a character. He was a good race driver. It was a shame he got killed. He was going to quit the year before the season he got killed, but didn't. It was such a good deal, and he made pretty good money, so he went on. That happened to a lot of people. He got burned pretty bad, but if it had been now, he would never have died.

Q.—He wasn't wearing a fire suit, was he?

A.—No. They didn't have fire suits then. Only problem was, he didn't have a safety fuel cell. What was in it [the car] was a lot stronger fuel tank. It was an iron pack plastic fuel cell, but when it hit the cement wall, it just busted. It just tore the whole car up. Then he was trapped inside the car somehow. We used to go down to see him when he was in the hospital. He liked Western music. He was dosed up, and he would sing these Western songs and go on. The nurse would say, "Be quiet. Do you want to kill yourself?" And he would say, "If I worried about that, I wouldn't be driving a race car." He was a character.

Q.—Were any of your drivers superstitious?

A.—Yes. David Pearson hated peanuts and green. He wouldn't touch either one. If you put peanuts in his race car, he wouldn't race. A lot of the guys hated snakes. My job was always to make sure the cars were built right before they left out of there. They were ready to leave. At the racetracks, we had six or eight or ten cars at the racetrack, and some of them weren't running. Ford was on your back: get them running. You'd have to go over, take a ride in it, find out what was the matter, including the chassis setup on it. Sometimes... I would get involved with jumping in so many cars, pretty soon I couldn't leave because I didn't know what I was doing. I was lost. I was going from one car to another to another. I had to go to all the races. But we'd go to places like Riverside or Daytona with six race car drivers. Every time you turn around, there was another car out there trying to find out what was wrong with it. Pretty soon, you'd get lost on where you were at, with so many cars and so many different things.

Q.—Did you expect Dan Gurney to do as well as he did the first time he drove a Ford at Riverside?

A.—Back then, that was a really funny thing. Dan got in the car and couldn't get around the racetrack. I could see what was wrong. He never drove anything that heavy. He knew how to drive sports cars, especially down through the esses, you know, accelerating from one corner to another, and he couldn't do that. He was really upset he wasn't running well. I showed him how to do it. It was a fact, he was mad, and he went home. Next morning, he wanted to come back. So we walked around, and I explained to him what he was doing wrong. He picked it up like that. To run a big car like that through the esses, you had to get to a speed that would carry you through them all. Not try to accelerate from this corner and stop and go to the next one. Just get a rhythm set and go through it. With a little, light car, you could accelerate from one corner to the next.

Dan was a heck of a road racer. He never liked Daytona or Atlanta. At that time, he was getting older, and he had never done anything like that. It was strange to him. He didn't spend enough time at it. We took him and Dick Rathman to Atlanta. We had a car, and the one that ran the fastest in practice was going to drive the car. They went out there and it was windy and neither one of them liked it. During Gurney's run, it was really windy out there. It didn't work, so I said, "Let me in it. I'll run it." I went a lot faster than either. Then I came back. Dick Rathman said, "Let me in." [I said,] "If you can run like that, you go racing." He said, "Hell, I can fly in that thing." So he went out there on the second lap and stuck it in the corner down the wall. Then we couldn't find him for about four hours. Then he came walking back in later. He said he was so embarrassed he didn't know if he was coming back.

Q.—If, through some magic, we could get the drivers from the sixties in their prime together with the current drivers in contemporary cars, how do you think guys like Fireball, Junior [Johnson], and others would stack up?

A.—If they could drive what they drove like they did, they can drive anything. They were just good race drivers. If they were here today driving this type of thing, they would be front-runners like they were then. They were just that type of people. They could get those sleds around back then, that weighed that much, without aerodynamics. They didn't have the tires. They didn't have a lot of stuff they have today. There is a lot more knowledge about what you are building, and the cars are even safer. But the guys had the talent.

Q.—Can you name the best driver you saw in the sixties and early seventies?

A.—They were all good. That's why we had so many different ones in the cars we had. Mario Andretti—the first time we took him to Daytona, he won the race. That's the reason we had those kind of people. We could take one of them and put them in a car that you had control over, and everyone would be a winner. All those guys, if you put them in something you control, then you have a winner. The only thing that would stop them was a wreck or something unforeseen. They had the talent to run the car up front.

Winning races is not all pit stops. It is driving ability. Most racing is mental. You've got to consider you are sitting in a car that is closed up, it is 130 degrees. What little bit of air you get is like sitting in front of a sauna and getting blasted. For three hours, you have to sit there and concentrate. If you miss your point by a foot, you could be in the wall, or you could be messed up for laps trying to get your concentration back. That's the reason: Fred Lorenzen, Junior Johnson, and David Pearson concentrated on what they did for three hours. They weren't any braver or any better at going around a racetrack than any of them, but they had the mental capacity to sit there and think about what they were doing and not get distracted.

A lot of times, after a race, when I asked Roberts, "What happened to that guy who just about got into you?" He'd say, "What guy?" You don't see it. If something happens near a race car and you're so focused on what you are doing, you didn't know it. A guy might have slid right past you—within inches of you—but you never saw him. Because it wasn't something to contend with. Those are the reasons that good drivers like Dale Earnhardt are so hard to beat. Bill Elliott is one of those kind of guys. When he gets himself tuned in and focused on what he is doing and stays there all day, he's a hard man to handle.

Big thing you do with a race driver from the pits is keep after them all the time, especially now with the radios. We had the first radio with Bobby Allison in that Mercury. Before that, you had to keep after them with signs or waving your arms at them or something to keep them awake to what was going on. He's out there running, and all of a sudden he's 2 seconds off the pace or you aren't getting it done. You have to do something to wake him up so he gets back on course again. The radio is really good for that because you can talk to the guy, and you don't want him talking back to you unless he wants to. You tell him every three laps where he is running. It keeps him focused in on what he is doing when he is running. It doesn't bother him, and it helps him. He can realize something is wrong with his race car, he's running out of tires or something. It makes him think.

Q.—How about single overhead cam engines? Did you build any of those before they got outlawed?

A.—No.

Q.—Of all the race cars you were involved with, is there one that sticks out in your mind as being the most enjoyable, the most successful, the best? Or any that you were most fond of?

A.—There were so many of them. Sometimes we built 200-300 in one year.

Q.—Which was your favorite body style race car?

A.—Talladega was a nice one. They went fast and all that. A lot of other stuff did, too. Probably those years with Bobby Allison were the most fun we had. In 1971, we ran Bobby in a 1969 Mercury and won ten superspeedways with it. Didn't start him in it until after the Darlington race. We had a lot of fun that year with that thing. We had a lot of good race cars, and no one really sticks out in my mind that was better than another or anything else. The time we had Pearson in, we won a lot of races. Lorenzen, the same way, back when he was in it. All of the teams were good.

Today, hardly any body on the car is the way it's supposed to be. It's just sheet metal. You used to have to have the [production] body. Today, you don't have to. They just make it look like one. Before, they were good race cars, but now, they're nothing. You can't buy a Chevrolet with a Ford rear end in it. That's what most of them run. Everything is off the Ford. Most of that was made by Holman and Moody. In the days when the Talladegas were racing, the car was basically a shell from the firewall back. Everything was stock. The chassis that was made then was a front snout, which is the same snout used today on rear steer cars, with two rails down the sides to poke into the rocker panels. You passed your roll cage through the rocker panels down into the frame rails. Essentially, that's all the cars were. The back ends of the car were not built strong like they are today.

An old friend, Junie Donlavey, still laughs about a car I helped him with. He says it was the best car he ever had.

He wanted a new chassis, but he couldn't afford one, and he wasn't one of the guys who was on our giveaway list from Ford. So I slid a chassis out the backdoor to him just to help him out because Junie is a really good friend. He said, "I don't have any way to put it together. I don't have a jig or anything." So I said, "Do you have a level floor in your garage anywhere?" "Yeah, we got that," he said. I told him to lay it on a level floor. Stuff the frame back to the rocker panels with the cross-members on the floor, and weld it. That's all a jig is anyway: a level floor. Junie took it home and did it. He never thought the thing would run at all. He ran it as long as he could. He claimed it was the best car he ever had.

But that's the difference today. Today, for $8,000 to $9,000, you get a car that was made on a surface plate, and every piece of it is precision made. Yet they don't run that much better. Hardly better at all. Look at the speeds the Talladega ran and the speed at the last Daytona race. Not a lot of difference. Take a car like the Talladega. It had to sit 6in off the ground. If you had a car today that sat 6in off the ground, they'd laugh at you. The tires they ran in those days were 8in max—and as hard as that table. No spoiler. Nothing. And they run 200mph. They ran 195 back in '69. Those are average speeds. The track speeds at the end of the backstretch at Daytona and Talladega were in excess of 225mph at Talladega. You actually had to get on the brakes going into Daytona corners. The deal was, they ran them flat on the floor. They leave pit road, foot on the floor. Come back in when they need gas again and lift the throttle. Today, it is totally different from what it was in those days. Yet they don't drive that much faster.

Q.—You've mentioned the Talladegas several times now. From where did the idea come for that car?

A.—Well, the place that all came about was Detroit, in engineering up there. I was up there with those people, working with them on what to do. They've got an engineering department up there. They'll have every car on the market in that place. And lots of room to work. We just kept swapping stuff around on cars to see what it would look like. We tried the back bumper on the front, for example.

Q.—So who actually came up with the idea for the extended fenders?

A.—It was a guy I worked with up there. A guy in the engineering building who oversaw things. I don't remember his name. But he just had more than he could do. That's why they wanted me up there. A couple of guys over in the shop and I just got to swapping things around. The first Talladega we fixed was made out of there. We took it over to the "Glass House," where all the big wheels are, one day and showed it to them. They thought it was neat.

Q.—What about the car we've heard you put together at Holman and Moody? It's been widely reported that you put together a stretch-nosed Torino that had Cyclone fenders. Is that true?

A.—Oh, yes, we fooled around with some of that in Charlotte. Then we went up there [Dearborn] and put one together. We started cutting stuff up. Like the bumpers. We sent to Atlanta [Ford's Fairlane assembly plant] and got the stuff. The noses and all that stuff.

Q.—So, that was the car that [Jacques] Passino came to look at the day that Dodge unveiled the Charger 500 at Charlotte?

A.—Yes.

Q.—From what you've said, though, the first Talladega was the one you put together in Dearborn?

A.—Well, I had a couple of guys in my place, and there were a couple more guys up there. We were all working on it. There wasn't that much to it. We took a black Torino and put both ends on it. We made the fenders up out of metal extensions. We lowered it. It was quite a nice-looking car. We also made a notchback. Ford said the notchback would run faster than a fastback. No way.

Q.—So, you actually put a Talladega-style nose on a notchback?

A.—Yes. We took them to Daytona. But the notchback just wasn't in the same class. At 150mph, it would run easier than the fastback. When you got over that, the fastback was gone.

Q.—Was that the first Talladega test?

A.—No. I set the first chassis up, and we went to Atlanta. We didn't take it to Charlotte because we didn't want people to know what we were doing.

Q.—Did you build all, or at least some, of the racing Talladegas at Holman and Moody?

A.—That's right. When we put them together, we put them together smaller, too. There was a 1/2in variation on the panels. What we'd do is use up that variation in the seams and make the whole car smaller. When they would sit next to a Torino in my shop, you could see they were smaller.

Q.—Did you build some of the Talladega fender extensions in your shop, too?

A.—We had a machine that made that stuff. We sold that stuff to people all over.

Q.—Compared to the other race cars that you built, was the Talladega one of the better cars?

A.—Yes. It was a nice handling car. It was a super car on account of what it was—you know, the fastback design. The only problem was, we had it too high off the ground.

You couldn't run a real spoiler on it. There was a little rear deck with a lip around it, but it didn't amount to much. If we could have run front spoilers and rear spoilers like today, the thing would have been dynamite. You didn't have to stop it when you got to the corners at 140.

Q.—A car called the King Cobra was supposed to replace the Talladega in 1970. Who designed it?

A.—Ford did that. They played with it awhile.

Q.—But Holman and Moody did some King Cobra testing, right?

A.—Yes. We pulled the nose down because there was no rear spoiler. We tested it with [a] spoiler on it at Atlanta. Man, would it fly. Cale [Yarborough] drove it for us. Later, we ran it at Daytona.

Q.—Do you recall how large a rear spoiler you had to use?

A.—Maybe a 3in spoiler or something like that. But they never went anywhere with that thing. NASCAR wouldn't let them run it because it was too streamlined. I put those snouts on three cars after I got out of Holman and Moody. I wound up with about four noses, and I sold them.

Q.—Let's talk about the evolution of the Holman and Moody chassis. When did the four-sidebar cage come into use?

A.—It was in '68. We gutted the door, took the hinges off. We used to have the hinges on, and you put the Bondo up over them so they would hold together. Some took the hinges off and put three rails high on the side. They made us take it home and cut all that out and put a stock door back on. Then we went to Atlanta a little bit after that. Then NASCAR decided that was a good idea and that we could

Fred Lorenzen was one of the first drivers signed by Holman and Moody after Ford decided to reactivate its factory-backed racing efforts. The choice was a good one, and Lorenzen went on to win 26 Grand National victories during his time on the circuit in cars like his H & M–prepped 1962 Galaxie. As you can see, coefficient of drag was of little concern in Detroit circa 1962. Craft Collection

reinforced factory control arms. Before that time, we had to use stock Galaxie arms. Then we tried making them out of tube, at least the upper arms. The lower ones still had to be reinforced Galaxie pieces. I remember in '69 that we built a separate Pearson car [a Torino Talladega] that had Heim joints. It was fully adjustable. They let me run it one race. Then we couldn't run it again. They made me weld it up. I had it where you could adjust the camber right there and lock it down. They wouldn't let us do that.

Q.—What about the rest of the front suspension and steering gear? How stock were mid-sixties Grand National cars in this area?

A.—Well, the spindles were heavy-duty Holman and Moody. They had bigger bearings, bigger races, and everything like that. The tie rods were stock. So were the drag links. The strut rods used to be one piece, and then they put an adjuster in them. That was so we could adjust the wheelbase a little bit. Holman and Moody did that. The steering box was a Galaxie part, too. Sometimes we would change the internal ratio, though.

Q.—When you first got into racing, most stock cars had leaf spring rear suspensions. Newer cars carry coils over the rear housing and are fully adjustable. How did you set up a non-adjustable rear leaf spring suspension for racing?

A.—We did have adjusters in some cases back in the sixties. That was about '62 or '63. Before that, we just put more arch in the spring. If we wanted more bite in the left rear, we just put a little arch in that spring. It wasn't easy, but that's what we did. Some guys also ran reversed spring eyes on one side or the other. I never did do that, but it was done. We couldn't get it down to a minor, minute thing [adjustment] like you can now. It was hard, because you couldn't change it during a race. Whatever you adjusted in practice, was what you raced. Now they change that in nothing flat. But back then, we were not equipped.

Q.—What about the floating rear hubs that came into widespread use during the sixties? Did Holman and Moody come up with that idea, too?

A.—I can't say who developed them. There was a man in Iowa, in '59, who developed a spindle that would slide over the stock spindle and bolted on. That got you bigger bearings and stuff in the front. Then he developed a free-floating hub on the rear. The rules book said they were optional. In fact, at first, you still had to run the axle that had a flange at that time. But if the axle broke, the wheel didn't come off 'cause you had a floating hub.

Q.—We know that most of your experience was with Fords. What was your impression of the torsion bar front suspension that Mopar racers of your era, like Richard Petty, used? Petty has said that torsion bars were difficult to set up on race day.

A.—Well, I can see where it would be because you had to change the torsion bar. With coil springs, you could just throw a spring in there in a few minutes. But the Mopar guys were tough. I would say that Chrysler probably had a better engineering department—as far as racing goes—than Ford did. Ford was hit and miss at the race car track, where Chrysler had engineers that were pretty sharp on all that stuff. They did a lot of work.

Q.—What about roll cage construction? Early NASCAR rules books only specified one sidebar, for example. When did the four-sidebar-style cages come into use?

A.—I was going to say it was about '64 when we started using the side-door bars. It's hard to remember, but I was thinking '64 or '65 when we started using them. You know, at one time, the doors opened. They had the original hinges in there. We just bolted them shut.

Q.—The Galaxies that you drove in '65 rolled on full,

factory-style frames. Later in the sixties, unit-body Fairlanes began to show up. What was done to a unit-body car's chassis to prepare it for, say, 500 miles at Daytona?

A.—The Fords started using unit bodies in '66 and '67. Bud Moore ran a Comet in '66. Curtis Turner ran a Fairlane, too, in '66. I think the first place we ran one was at Hickory. That's when Ralph [Moody] came up with the subframe deal. Most of us had boycotted in '66 [owing to NASCAR's refusal to permit the 427 overhead cam engine] and that's when Moody came out with the subframe to put on that unit body. They used a '65 Galaxie chassis, rewelded everything, and then attached it to the car with rails that ran down the rocker panels. That's what we all ran in '67 when we went to the smaller cars.

Q.—So, the rear of a "half-chassis" car was a mostly stock production unit body, then?

A.—Pretty much. We had to reinforce the front spring mounts. We also had to add the cage and the rear shock mounts. The floor pan was mostly the same except where we mounted things like the dry-sump reservoir and the fuel cell.

Q.—When did the NASCAR rules book permit the use of a fully fabricated front clip?

A.—Seems like that was somewhere in 69. [John] Holman talked NASCAR into letting us make up the snouts out of square tubing. That was easier than rewelding Galaxie rails. It really just made things easier to fix after a wreck.

Q.—How different are the fabricated snouts that are used today on the Winston Cup circuit from the ones that Holman and Moody started making in '69?

A.—They really weren't that different at all until the front steer cars started getting popular.

Q.—How long did unit-body cars remain on the circuit?

A.—Well, Plymouths and Dodges were unit-body cars right along. The Fords stayed unit-body until the early seventies.

Q.—What happened then?

A.—First the cars went from leaf spring rears to coils.

Q.—When was that?

A.—1972. Full frames came back at the same time under the Fords.

Q.—In that case, did you use the full Ford frame, or did NASCAR permit the use of a fully fabricated chassis?

A.—No, we had to use stock side rails and all. We had to tie the fabricated front end into the Ford rails.

Q.—How long did that last? When did you make the transition to the purpose-built frames that are run today?

A.—I don't know when we started putting the box tubing on the side rails. They let us do the tubular rear end before they let us change. We still had to use the stock side rails from the factory.

Q.—So the change was made in increments, then.

A.—Right. Then you're getting up on into the late '70s, 'cause I remember, in '75 and '76, when we were running Chevelles, we still had to run those stock side rails. We had to take a frame just to get the stock side rails. Then we could put a tubular front and back on them. But we still had to use those stock side rails. Someplace, they let us start boxing them in. Then they said, we'll just go to the coil. But I'm not sure what year that was.

Q.—Trailing arms to locate the differential were obviously part of the coil spring package. Were those stock pieces, or did you specially fabricate them like you do on modern cars?

A.—Depended on the time. In '65 and '66, we used little, short Ford trailing arms on our coil spring cars. Actually, they were Galaxie trailing arms. That's what we used on our Holman cars. Not everybody did that. In '65, Junior

Johnson put Chevrolet truck trailing arms under his car [also a Galaxie]. I remember that because Junior let me drive one of his cars on a north trip we took that year. We used to go north after Daytona in July. He ran road courses and short tracks, too. The car Junior let me drive had the long trailing arms.

Q.—It's been said that Junior first got the idea to use long trailing arms when he was driving his Mystery Motor Impala during '63. He liked them so much that he continued to put them on all the rest of his race cars, including the Galaxies he drove during the mid-sixties. Was he the first builder to do that?

A.—Yes. He also had a straight panhard rod like they run at Indy on the back, too. From Ford, we had a Watts link on the back [in our Galaxies]. He told me, "When you run this thing off the corner and it feels like it's gonna get loose, just stand back in it and it will stick." And it worked.

Q.—The Watts link you mentioned was originally made out of tie rod ends, wasn't it?

A.—It got better after a while, but basically, that's what they were made out of.

Q.—So, the Chevy truck-style trailing arms and panhard rods that Hutcherson-Pagan and the other major race car shops use today are basically what Junior Johnson started using during the sixties?

A.—Pretty much.

Q.—When did the 9in Ford differential that those arms are used to locate today become the "industry standard" in NASCAR?

A.—Well, Chrysler mostly used their own stuff, but we've been using the 9in since '60 to '61. In fact, it was a Mercury, a big Mercury rear end. It had the 9in. Holman introduced the nodular chunk around the same time, and they also developed what people call the Daytona Pinion support.

Q.—What about the Chevrolet racers of the period? What differentials were they using?

A.—I can't truthfully answer that. I'd say they were running the 9in. Chrysler guys, like Harry Hyde, used their own stuff for years, though.

Q.—It sounds like the NASCAR rules book in the sixties wasn't all that specific about the origin of parts.

A.—You did whatever you could get by with.

Q.—What about front suspension and steering gear? The rear steer cars that are still running in Winston Cup look to be using '65 Galaxie-derived parts even today.

A.—That's correct. They still use the Galaxie lower control arm, but they have to box it. Tie rods and drag links are basically the same, too. Harry Gant's using the old Galaxie steering boxes, too, because he's got so many of them. They just drill their frames for them. We used to have to go to the junkyards to buy control arms because Ford wasn't making them any more. Then they started to again. Same thing with Galaxie steering boxes. They're getting hard to get. But that's not a big problem now that most guys are using front steer and Saginaw boxes.

Q.—What is the advantage of front steer over rear steer?

A.—I don't think there is any. It's just driver and crew chief preference. There isn't any big deal to running these cars. Just get the horsepower, the right driver, and the right crew chief setting it up.

Q.—Front steer cars carry the steering gear ahead of the axle centerline and, as a result, pull, rather than push, the critical right front wheel. Does that really make a big difference in the way a car handles?

A.—The front steer, from what the drivers say—I've never driven a front steer car—makes the car seem tight.

That means the back end seems loose. Some drivers, [Dale] Earnhardt, for example, like that.

Q.—Who was responsible for introducing front steer cars?

A.—Bobby Allison had a lot to do with that, probably because he was building his own Chevy race cars during the sixties. They used the front steer setup that they came with from the factory.

Q.—Turning now to brake evolution, we've read that the Holman and Moody drum brakes, which most sixties Grand National cars used, were based on Lincoln pieces. Is that correct?

A.—Lincoln, yeah. At first, we used stock drums and backing plates. Later they let us drill the backing plates for more cooling. We used full metallic shoes.

Q.—How well did that setup work?

A.—Depends on the track, like it does now. At Riverside, it was hard to keep brakes in the car. We had adjustables on them so we could make adjustments. Where on a street car you have to back up to adjust the [drum] brakes, we turned them around and cut every other notch out of them, so they would adjust when the car was going forward. It got squirrely. By the end of a race, you had to be careful.

Q.—You mentioned that at first, stock backing plates were used. Later drum brake cars used fabricated mounts for the shoes, referred to by many people as "spiders." Who was responsible for that innovation?

A.—I think that was something else that [Ralph] Moody did. The spiders were stronger, and they allowed a lot more air to get in there.

Q.—Disc brakes came next? It's widely held that Roger Penske and Mark Donohue's AMC Matador was the first NASCAR effort to run disc brakes. True?

A.—When I had already turned my resignation in at Holman and Moody, I was talking with Penske about building that car, but I wasn't open to start on the work. They did that at Holman and Moody. But, yeah, Donoko was the first with disc brakes.

Q.—Did that change meet with any resistance from NASCAR?

A.—I don't think he had too much hassle on that. I didn't like it because it was different from what we'd been running. If it ain't broke, don't fix it. Those brakes were something off of a Trans-Am car or Formula One car that Penske sent us down to put on. They weighed about 3lb less than the drum setup. We had problems with the brakes at Riverside because we had to change the pads during the race, and we didn't have any extras. Penske used the discs first.

Q.—Were those discs based on a stock setup, or were they pure race?

A.—I'd say they were from one of Donohue's sports cars. Mark was pretty sharp.

Q.—How quickly did the rest of the NASCAR field change over to discs after Penske introduced them?

A.—I'm trying to remember when Moody came over with them. I don't really remember. Basically, teams just decided to change on their own. The discs were a lot lighter and a lot better—a lot better brake.

Q.—We've noticed that many current NASCAR cars still use the same single-reservoir master cylinder that has been in use since the early sixties. Why? Is that in the rules?

A.—No, you can run dual cylinders with a bias bar, if you want. The old Ford truck cylinder has a pretty good distribution, front to rear, so a lot of drivers still run them. They don't have to mess with it, just bolt it on and go.

Q.—What type of brake fluid is used in a Winston Cup car's system?

A.—We use the DOT stuff.

Q.—As brake systems evolved in NASCAR racing, so, too, did the wheels and tires. Early Grand National cars seemingly used stock rims. Where did they come from?

A.—We used to buy them from, seems to me, Quincy Steel, in Quincy, Illinois. They put them on agricultural implements or trucks. Then Holman welded the center in.

Q.—The slotted, Norris Industries wheel began to show up on cars in the early seventies. Why was the change made away from the Holman and Moody rims?

A.—To provide better cooling and to get more clearance for the disc brakes.

Q.—During the sixties, treaded racing tires were still being used. Judging from period photographs, that continued into the seventies. When was the transition made to the treadless slicks used today?

A.—I remember that one year we went to Talladega and had a lot of problems with tires. That was in '69, at the first race there. We were still on treaded tires then. But I don't remember exactly how much longer we ran tread on the tires; [probably] into the seventies.

Q.—You've said the cars you drove when you first broke into NASCAR racing were pretty stock. How much did you change the bodies in those days?

A.—Not much, really. At the time, we were still using regular production body panels, complete cars, actually. As we went along, we were allowed to remove more and more pieces, side trim and all of that. But at first, the cars were pretty close to stock.

Q.—How about the cars you build today? How stock are they?

A.—The rules today only require that a car's roof and deck lid be standard production. Everything else on the body can be pretty much made-to-order. We stock most every body panel here in our warehouse to build a car. But most of those parts get completely worked over while they are going on a chassis. Of course, the whole nose cap on a car today is molded out of plastic to keep cleanup simple after a wreck. Back in the sixties, it took a long time to clean up after a wreck—'specially all that glass.

Q.—You had to run full side glass in those days, didn't you?

A.—That's right. They had to roll up and down, too. We did put Lexan in the rear window, though.

Q.—When did NASCAR drop the side glass requirement?

A.—Actually, side glass was optional in NASCAR since the early sixties. But most guys kept the glass in on the big tracks, at least, for aerodynamics. It wasn't until, I'd say, '71 or '72 that side glass was outlawed.

Q.—Why was that step taken?

A.—Safety. I think that David Pearson and Bobby Isaac were probably the ones who contributed to that, too. I know we didn't think about it back then, but with those windows, ain't no way anybody could get us out of there. I mean, you should have gotten claustrophobia in there.

Q.—How hot was it in the cars in those days?

A.—Hot. Fourth of July, we used to roll the right side down a little bit to let a little air in. When we got rid of the windows, we got more crush room for the cage, because then we were able to move the cage out. It was just a better deal all around.

Q.—How about the cars that you build today? How much of their greenhouse is glass, and how much is Lexan?

A.—The windshield is glass, of course. The back window is Lexan, and so are the side windows.

Q.—Is the windshield in a modern NASCAR car DOT stock, or has it been modified for racing?

A.—They are not exactly what you would put on your car because they've been shortened. The piece that hangs down below the hood on a modern car is 4in or 5in long. It just hangs down there and doesn't do anything. That part is cut off.

Q.—During the late sixties, you were on hand for the factory-backed aero-wars. During '69 and '70, Chryco and FoMoCo built a handful of specially bodied cars just to go racing on the Grand National circuit. You were the crew chief on David Pearson's Holman and Moody-backed Torino Talladega?

A.—That's right. I was also with David the year before, too, but that car was just a regular Torino.

Q.—Who was responsible for coming up with the sleek Talladega design?

A.—Ralph Moody. It was just hit and miss. He tinkered around in the back room at Holman and came up with the design. There wasn't all that much to it. In fact, Moody used a back bumper and put it on the front. He's the one who came up with the idea of cutting it down to fit in place.

Q.—What gave Moody the inspiration? Was the Talladega just a stroke of genius, or was it an answer to inside information about the new aerodynamic Charger 500s that were being built?

A.—That I can't remember. What I would say is that we probably had some knowledge of what was going to happen, so we had to do something. And really, the Talladega was just something that Ralph came up with using common sense. He was sharp on things like that. It was just a cobbled-up piece, but it worked. In fact, I think the Spoiler [Mercury's version of the Talladega] was a little better. The Spoiler had a little different hood design, and that made it run a little bit better. Pearson and I kept trying to get them to give us a Spoiler to race instead of a Ford. They said, "No. You're running a Ford team, not a Mercury team." But we knew the Spoiler looked better. We wanted every advantage we could get. But they would never let us have one. We won the championship that year anyway.

Q.—How did Pearson's Talladega stack up to its Charger 500 and Charger Daytona competition? According to the record book, Talladegas and Spoiler IIs actually won more long-track races than the winged Mopars they ran against. Did the Fords and Mercurys have an advantage?

A.—I don't think we had an advantage. They had a heck of an engine [the 426 Hemi]. I think it was pretty even. Those Dodges and Plymouths were tough. You better bring your lunch if you were gonna beat them, because it was gonna take all day.

Chapter 3

Racing into the Future: The Modern Era, 1972-1994

NASCAR's "modern era" began with the collapse of the factory-backed competition that had characterized the sixties. Ford was the first to pull up stakes and retreat to the economy car backwaters in 1970, following the ascension of Lido Iacocca to the corporation's penultimate penthouse. Chryco stayed in the fray but a season or so longer before folding its racing tent and stealing away from the circuit. By the end of 1972, Grand National stock car racing was basically back where it had started twenty-three years before, in terms of corporate sponsorship.

Car owners and drivers were pretty much left to their own devices, too. Racing factories like Holman and Moody and Petty Enterprises were suddenly without customers, and former factory team drivers were without rides. It was doubtless a scary and uncertain time for just about everyone involved in the sport. Fortunately, old-line teams like the Wood Brothers, Bud Moore, Richard Petty, and Junior Johnson were around to lend stability and provide guidance in the strange new world of "factory-less" stock car racing in the early seventies.

For Petty, Moore, and the Woods, carrying on in the absence of tankersful of factory money meant, at first, making the most of the parts left in the wake of that funding. In many cases, teams had enough parts stockpiled for years of competitive racing—assuming the NASCAR rules book didn't change with the frequency it had in the sixties.

Unfortunately, for most racers on the circuit, the NASCAR rules book seemed to change from day to day during the first three or four years of the modern era. Keeping up with each new revision while trying to keep a commercial sponsor happy drove many from racing. Even giant car maker Chrysler cited the sanctioning body's rules instability as part of the reason for its decision to withdraw from racing in 1972.

Most of the upheaval was directly related to the amount of horsepower a race-spec engine was capable of putting out. Beyond frequent changes to the sections governing carburetion and induction systems, the official rules book actually changed very little. Minimum weight dropped to 3,800lb in 1971, for example, and remained unchanged for the rest of the decade. The 115in (intermediate) to 119in (full-sized) wheelbase chassis permitted on the racing grid were equally unaltered all the way until 1981. The configuration of the typical

Grand National car's underpinnings actually became more standardized as the seventies progressed. In fact, when Ford intermediates returned to body-on-chassis construction in 1972, the basic configuration of the cars that today compete in the Winston Cup was set.

During the first part of the seventies, full-frame cars were permitted to graft a fabricated snout—quite similar to the one developed from the Galaxie line by Holman and Moody in 1965—onto the rest of their race car's full chassis. Later in the decade, a fabricated rear clip was also permitted, although at the time, the frame's original side rails still had to be retained. Finally, by the end of the decade, NASCAR tech officials permitted the use of a fully fabricated chassis similar to the one Smokey Yunick had been disqualified for running in 1966.

One significant chassis change that did take place during the seventies was the introduction of aftermarket disc brakes, front and rear. Though Grand National

Most Ford racers reverted to 1969 Mercurys when NASCAR handicapped the special aero-cars that had run in 1969 and 1970. Truth be known, the Cyclone body was a bit faster than its Ford corporate cousin. Bobby Allison drove a Holman and Moody–prepped 1969 Cyclone for Coca-Cola in 1971. Craft Collection

When the factories pulled their sponsorship out of NASCAR racing, many of the formerly big names on the circuit shrank significantly in size. Holman and Moody was particularly hard-hit by Ford's retreat. Though that "racing company" tried gamely to soldier on by building customer cars—such as this road course Torino prepared for Driver Bobby Unser, the last H & M car built, in fact—Holman and Moody did not long survive Ford's departure.

A full-house Boss 429 was at Bobby Unser's command as he took the last Holman and Moody–prepared Ford into battle in the Winston Western 500 at Riverside in January of 1973.

Bobby Unser's road course Torino carried an electrically driven transmission cooler on the passenger's-side floor-board, to keep the top loader from welding up during the road race at Riverside.

rules had permitted "spot or disc brakes" as early as 1967, no one made a serious attempt to upgrade a NASCAR car's typically lackluster braking ability until Roger Penske and Mark Donohue started campaigning an upstart AMC Matador in 1973. The four-wheeled disc brakes that their red, white, and blue number 16 "Rambler" sported at that year's season opener at Riverside proved to be the key to victory. After that road course win, long-time sports car racer Donohue said his car's disc setup "made the difference. I could carry the car deeper in the corners and that's what it takes on a road course." Donohue's impressive one-lap victory, scored at his first appearance on the circuit, no doubt attracted more than a little attention along pit road. Before the middle of the decade, just about every team had made the transition to disc brakes.

The Seventies: Slick as a Brick

In 1969 and 1970, Ford and Chrysler had pulled out all the stops in a battle of aerodynamics. The end result was a fleet of swoopy-looking cars that sliced through the wind like a hot knife through butter. However, all the lessons learned about wind resistance and drag during those two seasons seemed to have been forgotten by the middle of the seventies. The cars Motown was turning out seemed to have all the aerodynamic attributes of a brick. Fords were particularly hard-hit by the styling trend toward squared-off, formal silhouettes. The boxy

Bobby Unser's car also carried an auxiliary differential cooler on the rear floorboard, behind the driver's seat.

American Motors has never been a real force in NASCAR racing. In fact, until 1973, only one Nash driver had ever won a race on the circuit; that lone win came in 1952. All of that changed as a result of a collaboration between Roger Penske and American Motors in 1973. Mark Donohue won the first Riverside race that year—in a red, white, and blue striped Matador equipped with four-wheel disc brakes—and then Dave Marcis campaigned the car at selected races. In 1973, Bobby Allison signed on with AMC and Penske, and together, that troika went on to win four more races in 1974 and 1975.

Generally speaking, the cars built by the Big Three during the mid-seventies were anything but aerodynamic. The end result was a starting grid full of squared-off stock cars that were all as slick as bricks. Take, for example, the Monte Carlo that Rusty Wallace drove during one of his first years on the circuit. Not exactly what you might call a swoopy aero-warrior, eh?

Thunderbirds and Montegos that were legal for NASCAR competition were anything but aerodynamic, and the win-loss record showed it.

Dodge drivers were able to campaign the same basic Charger body, first introduced in 1971, all the way through 1977 owing to the combination of a long production run and a rules change in 1977 that permitted any given body style to race for four years instead of three. But time eventually ran out for that classic body style, and when it did, Chryco's days as a force in NASCAR racing were effectively over. Mopar stalwart Richard Petty gamely tried to make competitive the Magnum body style that replaced the venerable Charger, but that proved to be a task beyond even the estimable skills of Petty Enterprises. Late in 1978, Petty reluctantly bought a Monte Carlo and started racing a GM product for the first time since 1959.

Things were somewhat better for GM drivers in general and Chevrolet drivers in particular. The Chevelle body style that had begun to show up on the NASCAR circuit was far less boxy than its FoMoCo competition. In fact, the sloping roofline characteristic of the design was downright swoopy. The only fly in the ointment was a front grille line and pair of headlight openings that confronted the onrushing air at a perfect 90-degree angle. Chevrolet stylists cured that peccadillo in 1975 with the introduction of a new trim package called the Laguna S-3. The most important part of that package, as far as Chevrolet racers were concerned, was a sloping nose section and molded-in front bumper. The new aero-package was an immediate success on the circuit, and Benny Parsons drove an S-3 to victory in the Daytona 500. Cale Yarborough drove a Junior Johnson-prepped S-3 to two NASCAR Championships in 1976 and 1977, winning five long-track events—including the 1977 Daytona 500—in the process.

When NASCAR officials decided in 1978 that the S-3 was a bit too slippery for its own good, GM teams quickly switched to Oldsmobile Cutlass bodies that carried angled-off nose cones that were nearly as aerodynamic as the S-3's nose section. Cale Yarborough proved as much by winning the 1978 Daytona 500 in Junior Johnson's Cutlass, along with the Winston 500 at Talladega, the Gabriel 500 at Michigan, and the Southern 500 at Darlington. By season's end, Yarborough had used his Olds' aero-advantage to win his third straight national driving title—an unprecedented feat. Richard Petty put that same body style to work in 1979 and imi-

Ford reemphasized the importance of aerodynamics in 1983 when an all-new Thunderbird body was introduced. A second round of factory-backed aero-competition quickly heated up. And, just as during the 1969–70 season, some factories even produced special aero-warriors that *would not otherwise have ever been built. The sleek new Thunderbirds and Luminas that make up most of a typical race's starting grid are still battling one another for aerodynamic supremacy. FoMoCo*

Significant Car of the Period
Things Go Better with Coke—
and with Chevrolet, Too

In 1971, Junior Johnson, as he often had in the past, set out in an entirely new direction. Though a Ford driver and team owner since 1964, Johnson and partner Richard Howard broke with the blue oval and assembled the parts necessary to field a competitive Chevrolet team. He also took advantage of the disintegration of Holman and Moody's racing fortunes to assemble a supercrew of experienced NASCAR veterans. Notable in that number were legendary crew chief Herb Nabb and a fresh-faced former Holman and Moody engine builder named Robert Yates.

The Monte Carlos that Nabb set up for drivers like Charlie Glotzbach and Bobby Allison were built over full chassis that reflected the increasing homogenization of the Grand National stock car. A Ford-developed 9in differential equipped with Holman and Moody-derived floater hubs was bolted beneath the Chevrolet's bustle, for example. And it was located by a pair of the trademark truck arm-evolved trailing arms that Johnson had been installing under his cars since Mystery Motor days. At the bow, fully fabricated upper control arms—allowed by NASCAR since the middle of the 1969 season—worked in concert with reinforced lower A-frames, heavy-duty spindles, and a set of screw jack-adjusted coils, to keep the Monte Carlo's bumper sufficiently above the asphalt. Two shocks were still the order of the day along pit road, and so were Holman and Moody-developed 11in "backless" drum brakes. One other significant feature found under a Johnson Chevrolet was stock Chevrolet-style steering components. Though rear steer boxes, drag links, and spindles refined by Holman and Moody in the sixties would continue to be predominant along pit road until the nineties, the superspeedway suc-

cess enjoyed by Johnson's early-seventies Chevrolets was not lost on the competition.

Cubic inches were still sovereign in 1971 and 1972, and the NASCAR rules book allowed engines of up to 430ci. Johnson's Monte Carlos were powered by 427ci bow-tie big-blocks that had received Robert Yates' personal attention. Built around iron blocks with four-bolt main journals, the engines featured an open-chambered alloy head casting and a single 4150-style 850cfm Holley carburetor. The carburetor restrictor plates that NASCAR had put into use late in the 1970 season at Michigan continued to be a factor on the superspeedways at the sanctioning body's discretion. When they were not in place, a Yates-prepped big-block churned out somewhere in excess of 650hp at its intended 6900rpm to 7200rpm operating range.

With Bobby Allison in command of those horses, Johnson's Monte Carlo became a regular fixture at the front of the superspeedway pack—a first for Chevrolet since 1963. While teamed together, Allison and Johnson won six long-track events, including the prestigious Southern 500 in Darlington, and recorded nine other superspeedway top-ten finishes.

When Allison left the team in 1973 to strike out on his own, Cale Yarborough was hired to drive. Chevrolet's glory years on the NASCAR circuit had begun. In the absence of any substantial factory support for their Ford and Chryco rivals, and greatly aided by an ever wider backdoor at Chevrolet's high-performance warehouse, bow-tie drivers made the seventies and eighties their own. From 1972 to 1992, Chevrolet drivers won an incredible 43 percent of all NASCAR races held: 255 of 588. When you factor in the wins scored by corporate cousins Pontiac and Buick during the same period, General Motors dominance on the circuit becomes even more pronounced. It's a fact not likely to be soon repeated.

Junior Johnson became the first major team owner to return to Chevrolet after Ford's and Chryco's departure from racing in the early seventies. The Monte Carlos he built quickly *became the cars to beat on the circuit. Daytona Speedway Archives*

tated Yarborough by winning the Daytona 500 in February. Buddy Baker made it three for three for Olds when he won the 500 in 1980 in yet another Cutlass.

As NASCAR's third decade came to a close, boxy-looking race cars were still the order of the day and big-block power was just a distant memory. Even so, by 1979, qualifying velocities at Daytona and Talladega had climbed back to the mid- to high 190s. Faster times were ahead in the eighties, as a second factory aero-war was set to resume.

The Eighties and Early Nineties: Let's Get Small

The year 1981 was the one in which NASCAR decided to downsize. In 1977, NASCAR had made a rules change extending the operational life of a particular car's body style. At the time, it was an attempt to control the ever-escalating costs of Winston Cup racing, by permitting older cars—already paid for—to continue running. By 1980, that rules change had resulted in more than a few "old cars" along pit road, and NASCAR races were in danger of looking like used-car lots.

In 1981, the sanctioning body decided to change the complexion of stock car racing by reducing the legal wheelbase length for Winston Cup cars from 115in down to 110in. Though a 5in difference in length might seem to be trivial, especially since most of the mechanical components inside the perimeter of a chassis remained basically unaltered, it was a major change for car builders and drivers alike. Immediately after the close of the 1980 season, teams started the laborious process of building entirely new fleets of cars. For most organizations on the circuit, that meant assembling three to four all-new cars and skinning them in body styles that had never turned a lap at superspeedway velocities. To say the learning curve was steep is an understatement.

Since tread width was kept at 60in, no major changes were required on most of the suspension components that had been in use for the past decade. But optimally packaging them inside a new, smaller frame was a challenge.

No major drivetrain changes were in the offing, either. GM cars of all stripes continued to campaign corporate small block Chevrolet engines, and Ford teams relied on a diminishing number of 351 four-barrel Cleveland castings. Through the seventies and eighties, Chevrolet teams had enjoyed the benefits of a high-performance aftermarket parts industry that was seemingly set up exclusively to make go-fast goodies for the small-block Chevrolet engine. Pistons, cams, intakes, special head castings, and all manner of other parts were as close as the local United Parcel Service delivery person for Chevrolet racers. It was a different story entirely for Chryco and FoMoCo drivers. One principal reason that Richard Petty cited for his decision to quit Chrysler products in 1978 was the unavailability of high-performance parts. By the end of the seventies, the supply of parts left over from Chryco's racing efforts in the sixties was just about exhausted. Making the situation worse was the unwillingness of most aftermarket manufacturers to tool up to meet the need. Although specially made racing pistons could be obtained overnight for the small-block Chevy engine of your choice, the same piece for a 360 Mopar motor might just take months to get. It was an untenable situation.

Junior Johnson and Darrell Waltrip found the earliest success on the downsized post-1981 NASCAR circuit. The Mountain Dew Buick Regals the two campaigned won the Winston Cup Championship two years running. Craft Collection

Things were only marginally better for Ford racers. Like their Chryco counterparts, they, too, had been relying on a dwindling supply of parts left over from Ford's Total Performance years and regular production components from the early seventies. When the switch to small-block power led by Bud Moore quickly used up the available supply of four-bolt Cleveland blocks, for example, Ford racers had gone as far afield as Australia in search of viable replacements. In fact, it was discovered that the heavy-duty 351 blocks originally cast up for use in Aussie Falcons were actually sturdier than their stateside counterparts. Of course, just like made-in-the-USA parts, Australian Clevelands were equally out of production, making supplies scarce and prices dear. Though a few specialty manufacturers had cranked up to supply the needs of Ford NASCAR racers, the situation was far from the favorable one enjoyed by Chevrolet racers. All of that would change by the middle of the next decade, however.

The Aero-wars Revisited: Fly Like an Eagle

The biggest problem encountered by NASCAR teams as a result of downsizing was learning how to make their new, smaller cars handle. Early tests conducted by GM teams in December of 1980 quickly re-

The Chevrolet Monte Carlo was a force on the NASCAR circuit from 1971 to 1989. During that time, it became the winningest body style in NASCAR history. Of the 550 races run, Monte Carlo drivers won 95.

than-perfect, Darrell Waltrip did find the Regal body style slippery enough to win back-to-back Winston Cup titles. D. W. and other Buick drivers won fully forty-seven of the sixty-two races held in 1981 and 1982—the first such wins for that GM division since 1955, when Buick's only two other wins had been scored.

Thunderbirds became even sleeker after they were restyled in 1986, which was bad news for their GM rivals. The new beaks and bustles they supported made 210mph-plus speeds a walk in the park at Daytona and Talladega. Restrictor plates were the direct result of that performance.

Ford's new T-birds came on-line in 1983, but Ford teams were still laboring under the lack of high-performance parts. However, newfound corporate interest in motorsports came on-line at about the same time that new T-birds were showing up at the dealerships. Within two seasons, that long-dormant enthusiasm for corporate-backed racing would produce positive results. First, a new version of Ford's SVE, called Special Vehicles Operations (SVO), was formed, and soon thereafter, new parts designed for racing began to issue forth from Fo-MoCo foundries. New blocks were cast to replace long-in-the-tooth Australian units, and new cant valve heads were designed to replace the cut-and-paste 4-V Cleveland castings that Bud Moore had introduced in the early seventies. In 1985, Bill Elliott, Cale Yarborough, and Ricky Rudd scored fourteen victories for Ford—eleven, two, and one, respectively—the same number as Chevrolet and the most for the blue oval in a single season since 1969. Ford was definitely back in the racing business.

Chevrolet's answer to the new Dearborn threat had first been introduced in 1983 in response to Darell Waltrip's dominant Mountain Dew Buick. Taking a page from the same recipe book that Ralph Moody had followed in creating the Torino Talladega two decades before, Chevy engineers introduced a new swoopy nose cone for the Monte Carlo and called the resulting new car the SS. Surprisingly like Moody's earlier design, the new nose featured a cowcatcher-type front bumper, a flush-fitting grille, and a hoodline that met the grille at the rounded-off angle. The new beak was trim and efficient, and it worked. The only fly in the ointment contin-

Bill Elliott's 1987 Thunderbird was the fastest car on the circuit that season—and that's primarily due to its slippery aerodynamic shape. The T-bird line's sloped nose and raised bustle worked together to produce awesome performance when powered by sufficient horsepower.

ued to be the same squared-off roofline that had plagued GM drivers since downsizing took place in 1981. However, Chevrolet stylists went back to the drawing board following the 1985 season. When Monte Carlo teams showed up at Daytona in February of 1986, their cars sported an all-new sloping backlight that swept from the C-pillar nearly to the edge of the severely abbreviated deck lid—just like the backlight on Ralph Moody's Talladega. And just like the cars of that earlier aero-design, the new Monte Carlo Aero-Coupes immediately started proving their worth on the track.

Geoff Bodine won the Daytona 500 in his number 5 Aero-Coupe to start the season, but Bill Elliott's 205.039mph pole-winning speed served notice that the Ford Thunderbird body was every bit as fast as the newly beaked and bustled Chevrolet. Elliott underscored that point by running 212.229mph to snare the pole at Talladega four months later. Even so, by season's end, Chevrolet drivers had scored eighteen Winston Cup victories to Ford's five, and Dale Earnhardt was the series champion.

Pontiac stylists had also introduced a slicked-up version of the Grand Prix called the 2+2. Like the Aero-Coupe, the new Poncho featured a grafted-on backlight that greatly smoothed the car's roofline. A unique nose-piece was also part of the package, and to the eye, it looked impressively sleek. In fact, coefficient of drag (Cd) numbers for the two GM aero-variants and the "stock"-bodied Thunderbirds were all in the .25 to .3 range—impressive for a street car, let alone a wide-tired and be-spoilered racing machine. The problem for Ford and Pontiac drivers wasn't aerodynamics, or even horsepower. The simple reason they were unable to slow the Chevrolet juggernaut was numbers. At any given race during the 1986 season, fifteen to twenty of the cars on hand were usually Monte Carlos. In comparison, there usually weren't enough Ford and Pontiac drivers on hand to hold a softball game.

That numbers disadvantage continued into 1987 for Ford drivers, but stylists had been hard at work back in Dearborn in an attempt to make up that deficit. Their answer was an all-new skin for the Fox-chassied Thunderbird, one that was even sleeker than the version that had been introduced in 1983. More a styling evolution than a revolution, the new cars featured revised nose panels that dropped more rapidly toward the pavement,

The Ford Thunderbirds and Chevrolet Luminas that currently dominate NASCAR's win column are undoubtedly

some of the sleekest and fastest NASCAR race cars ever to grace a racing grid.

The construction of a modern Winston Cup race car begins when lengths of square and round seamless tubing are cut to length. The current rules book specifies a minimum wall thickness of 0.12in.

cars—and, as a result, still prefer them—have all retired, 1965 Galaxie steering boxes and suspension components will become part of NASCAR's past just as have Boss 429 engines and treaded bias-ply racing rubber.

Once the basic chassis for today's GM and FoMoCo cars has been formed, the roll cage is added. Current rules require the use of seamless 1 3/4in round tubing, and the position of nearly every bar in the assembly is specified. The end result is a rigid framework that provides both unexcelled driver protection and unparalleled rigidity. Safety and handling are both beneficiaries of NASCAR's very stringent roll cage rules.

Suspension components come next. Even though the steel front A-frames are derived from seventies Camaro pieces, consumer cars share only their bushings and basic geometry with the custom-fabricated control arms used in a modern stock car. Custom wound springs, screw jack-mounted spring perches, a single pair of gas-pressurized shocks, and a through-the-frame composite sway bar all act directly on the fabricated con-

Winston Cup frames are assembled on surface plates—like the one shown here at Hutcherson-Pagan—to ensure accurate alignment of all critical suspension mounts.

High-quality inert-gas welding is used throughout the process.

The subframes that actually mount a Winston Cup chassis' suspension components are fabricated in a jig before being added to the full chassis.

Other than differences in steering style, front or rear, modern NASCAR chassis are today pretty much identical—regardless of the car make they might be used under. That's why chassis builders are able to stockpile snouts and other chassis components for future use instead of having to have separate Ford and GM inventories.

Once the roll cage and inner panels are added, a Winston Cup chassis begins to take on an identifiable shape. The specific "gender" of these two cars under construction at Hutcherson-Pagan will not become evident until they have received Ford or GM sheet metal.

Suspension mounts are of obviously critical importance All modern Winston Cup chassis use front-mounted coils that ride in screw jack–adjustable spring cups.

trol arm. Since the late eighties, most Winston Cup cars have carried power steering-plumbed Saginaw boxes that mount ahead of the front axle's centerline. A purpose-built drag link and tie rods work in coordination with custom-fabricated, removable pitman arms and heavy-duty spindles to dial in directional changes. Those steering inputs come through a U-joint-equipped steering column and a padded steering wheel that's been fitted with a quick-release coupling.

The rear suspension is built of a coil spring-suspended 9in Ford differential. Long-style Chevrolet pickup-derived control arms that angle forward from the third member to a chassis cross-member almost directly under the driver's seat govern longitudinal movement. A cross-chassis panhard rod carried directly behind the differential is used to keep lateral motion in check, and lengths of chain control vertical suspension travel. As at the bow, custom wound coils ride in screw jack-adjustable perches. They seat in cups on the trailing arms just ahead of the differential. Another feature shared with the front suspension is a single pair of gas shocks.

Brakes, Wheels, and Tires

The disc brakes used to stop a contemporary Winston Cup stock car are light-years ahead of the drums and shoes that once predominated on the circuit. Provid-

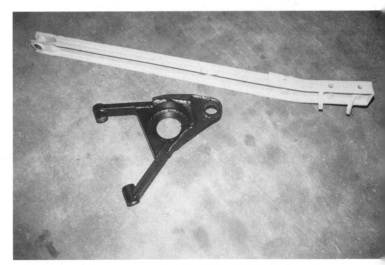

Suspension components are today fully fabricated and owe only their original geometry to any given manufacturer. Front steer cars, for example, employ handmade lower control arms derived from the Camaro line. The long trailing arms currently used under Winston Cup cars to locate the differential were originally found under Chevrolet trucks.

When in assembled form, the components of a contemporary Winston Cup car's front steer suspension look like this. Note the fully fabricated upper and lower control arms, the beefy spindle, the steering arm, the heavy-duty hub, and the ventilated disc brake. The dangling Heim joint assembly connects with the front sway bar's side arm.

ed by a number of aftermarket suppliers, the disc-and-caliper combinations in use today are track specific. Short-track and road course events require the use of beefy 1 1/4in-wide ventilated discs and multi-piston (up to six) calipers, whereas superspeedway races are often run with lighter components that don't need the extra bulk required on the bullrings. Brake technology is such that, barring a hydraulic failure, a single set of pads normally lasts an entire race and provides acceptable performance until the checkered flag is dropped. Pressure for that performance is provided by either a single-reservoir Ford truck-derived master cylinder or a pair of balance bar-adjusted remote reservoir units of more modern origin—depending on driver preference. In either case, braking is not power assisted.

Heavy-duty hubs, front and rear, carry a quartet of aftermarket 15x9.5/4.5in offset rims and Goodyear radials. The rolling chassis that results is next fitted with the sheet metal bodywork and drivetrain components that make it into one of the marques that currently compete on the circuit. Normally, only the way those components are mounted and plumbed distinguishes one team's car from another's.

Bodywork and Interiors

A current Winston Cup car's body is built up from a combination of stock OEM stampings and handmade panels formed on an English wheel—with a heavy emphasis on the latter. It is common for the hood skin, roof skin, and rear deck lid all to be pretty much the way they came from an OEM stamping plant. But beyond that, each team varies as to how much of the rest of its car is actually stock. Even so, its handiwork must at least look stock—as defined by NASCAR's templates, that is.

Starting with the single over-the-car templates introduced soon after the controversy surrounding Smokey Yunick's 15/16-scale Chevelle and Junior Johnson's *Yellow Banana* in 1966, NASCAR's templates have grown progressively more numerous and complicated. Today, fourteen official templates are used to govern a car's cosmetic appearance, and current rules allow only a quarter's thickness in deviation from them in most cases. A one-time, one-place 1/2in deviation is permitted from the all-important over-the-car template. How teams place that allowed amount of deviation and what they do in the areas between the other thirteen plates

Ahead of the Curve: Bud Moore's Small-block

In contrast to the old-style unit-body race car that Leonard and Glenn Wood campaigned for the first few years of the seventies, Bud Moore opted to run a new, full-chassis Torino on his return to the circuit after three years of running a Mustang-based Trans-Am team. The new-for-1972 Ford and Mercury intermediate lines rolled out of the factory on full-perimeter frames instead of the unit chassis of the preceding years. As a result, Moore was rules mandated to utilize a similar setup under his race car.

Fabrication began with the fitting of a tube-frame front snout quite similar to the ones in use since mid-1969. A-frames derived from the 1965 Galaxie and a rear steer Galaxie box were still part of the Ford chassis program, as were screw jack-adjustable coils and an H & M-style sway bar.

Though things were little changed at the bow of Moore's Ford, the car's rear suspension was all-new for 1972. A 9in third member still served as the rear suspension's principal player, but it was now located by a set of coil springs and the same Chevy-style trailing arms that Junior Johnson had been using since 1963. A cross-chassis panhard rod kept everything centered up, and a de rigueur quartet of shocks was used in concert with a similar number of dampers carried at the bow.

Another big difference between Moore's car and others on the circuit was the small-block 351 Cleveland mounted beneath its hood. The introduction and development of the Ford Boss 429 had taken place during Moore's

Though 1972 marked the return of the full chassis to the Ford line, cars like Bud Moore's small-block–powered Torino still relied on the same fabricated front snouts that had been in use essentially since 1966.

years on the Sports Car Club of America (SCCA) circuit. As a result, he had had little experience with it. He was, on the other hand, more than a little familiar with what it took to make a cant valve-headed Ford small-block run, since that was the engine his team's Boss 302 Mustangs had used for power. When it became apparent that the Boss 429's fortunes would only continue to wane on the circuit owing to the restrictor plate rule, Moore took the obvious

The 1972 Torino that Bud Moore built for Bobby Isaac to run in 1972 was one of the first to rely on small-block motorvation.

In contrast to the basically unchanged front suspension found under full-framed Fords starting in 1972, things were quite different at the rear. Coil springs returned to the program for the first time since 1966, for example, and long Chevrolet truck–style trailing arms worked in conjunction with them to locate the rear housing. Mike Slade

step of developing a NASCAR-spec small-block to power the Torinos he built for Bobby Isaac. When topped with an unrestricted Holley 1040 carburetor, a Bud Moore Mini-Plenum intake manifold, and a pair of the high-port heads he'd cooked up in his own shop, a Moore Cleveland could be counted on to produce in excess of 650hp—which, coincidentally, was actually a bit more than a restricted Boss 429 was capable of.

NASCAR's interest in promoting the use of small-block engines was readily apparent in the leeway that was allowed Moore in the cylinder head department. Though the four-barrel closed-chamber Cleveland heads he used on his car had, at one time or another, come out of a factory casting box, they were light-years away from stock by the time they hit the high banks. Most notable of the myriad modifications conducted on each head casting was the complete machining away of the original exhaust manifold surface. In fact, a 2x1in slice of meat had been taken out of the whole head surface, eliminating most of the stock exhaust runners in the process. A piece of aluminum was then bolted into place and finish machined with four new exhaust passages that terminated far higher than stock. The idea was, of course, to increase exhaust flow—a notorious shortcoming on most stock Ford small-block heads. Moore's crew took 34 work hours to finish off each head, and the process reportedly produced 20 extra horsepower. A Ford top loader four-speed and nodular chunk rounded out the drivetrain.

Moore's Torino proved its viability by beginning to score top-ten finishes as soon as it hit the starting grid. Greater success was hampered by a less-than-slippery aerodynamic profile (the car's gaping oval grille no doubt acted like an open parachute at speed) and by Isaac's decision to retire from racing during the 1973 season (actually, during the middle of the 1973 Talladega 500, where he radioed in to an astonished pit crew that he was coming for a pit stop to quit racing!).

Even though Moore's Torino didn't visit victory lane, it was a harbinger of things to come. Two short years later, nearly every car on the circuit was powered by some kind of small-block engine and a full-frame chassis with four coil springs.

Bud Moore, standing, has always been an innovative car builder. He was the first Ford racer to try downsizing to a FoMoCo intermediate in 1966, for example. In 1972, he became the first car builder on the circuit to turn to small-block engines for power when restrictor plates made big-block engines into a dying breed.

Ford's 9in differential has been a universal fixture in the NASCAR ranks since the last Chryco racer retired from the fray. Long trailing arms and a panhard rod are used to keep the unit centered under the chassis. Track-specific coil springs and a pair of gas-charged shocks are used both to provide and to control suspension movement.

determine a given car's aerodynamic profile. Super-speedway and intermediate-track cars, obviously, receive the most attention in this critical area. But the level of competition is such that even short-track cars are carefully built with aerodynamics in mind. Manufacturers like Ford commonly spend 160 to 200 hours per year in the wind tunnel with the different teams they are helping to support. The end result is a car that looks stock from the stands while scything through the air far better than anything in the parking lot outside.

In recent seasons, increasing speeds have caused the sanctioning body to take steps to slow cars down aerodynamically, in addition to the rules written about restrictor plates. In 1992, larger rear deck spoilers were mandated and their angle was fixed at 45 degrees, for example.

Ground clearance is closely monitored, and at present there must be at least 3.5in between the bottom of the spoiler and the racing surface. All Winston Cup cars must also carry roof panels that are no lower than 50.5in off the ground. Side skirts, lip rails on the roof, and enclosed passenger's-side windows all became mandatory equipment after a series of potentially fatal accidents in the late eighties that caused cars to become airborne at speed. Rules being formulated as this book goes to press in 1993 would limit front spoilers to an ex-

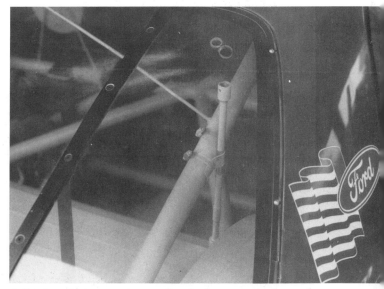

Adjustments to a car's rear "wedge" are made through small access holes that NASCAR allows teams to cut through the Lexan backlights in their race cars. The socket extensions connect to screw jacks mounted over each rear spring.

Disc brakes are used front and rear on a modern stock car. Drilled or ventilated discs, alloy "hats," and lightweight calipers make up the typical rear disc system. Note the single-stage cooling pump mounted on this "fully dressed" rear axle assembly.

In contrast to the often-inadequate drum brake systems common in the early days of NASCAR racing, state-of-the-art disc brake technology carries modern Winston Cup cars into battle. Multipiston calipers and massive, ventilated discs are used to haul hurtling stock cars down from speed. Interestingly, though, a good many teams still use Ford Galaxie single-cylinder master cylinders to pressurize their cars' braking systems.

Teams along pit road marshall their inventory of racing rubber just prior to a race. Tire pressure and diameter are critical to good handling.

Stamped-steel Ford-Fox chassis floor pans are used in all NASCAR cars today.

tension no more than 1/2in ahead of the bumper, in a further attempt to limit speeds by controlling a car's aerodynamic package. The struggle between the sanctioning body and the teams in this area is certain to continue for years to come.

With the body in place, the rest of the car's "interior appointments" can be fitted. A 22gal fuel cell takes up most of the available trunk space and is housed in a closely measured steel container. It is fitted with a dry-break filler neck that permits a full 22gal load of gas to be added in as little as 8 to 10 seconds. Current rules require mounting of the engine's dry-sump tank in either the driver's compartment or the trunk, so many teams place that 1,115ci reservoir adjacent to the fuel cell.

Another fabrication step taken in the trunk compartment is the construction of inner fender crush panels that extend from the wheelwell out to the body skin. Silicon is used to seal the crush panels to the body.

At the bow, aluminum panels are used to direct cooling air from radiator and bumper openings to the radiator and oil coolers. Winston Cup cars do not use inner fender panels over their front tires. Sheet steel firewalls are used at the front and rear of the driver's compartment to seal out engine heat and combustibles in the event of a fuel cell rupture. The rest of a car's interior is covered in textured aluminum panels primarily for cosmetic appearance. "Ergonomic appointments" consist of a single custom-fitted bucket seat, a steel panel dash, heat-resistant floor blankets, and the bulk of a car's ignition system. Cars slated to race in summer events are often fitted with the gear necessary for a driver cool suit, too.

Trimmed safety glass windshields are required in Winston Cup racing at the front of a car's greenhouse. Lexan side windows and backlights fill up the remaining openings.

Each piece of the car's body is held in place by a combination of metal straps and braces. Once the body-

work has been roughed into shape and fitted with the molded plastic nose and tail cones required by the rules book—to speed cleanup following shunts—it's time for a final fit and finish. That requires a liberal application of Bondo. In days gone by, a team might actually slather the whole car in a coating of plastic 1/8in thick. That is changing, however, as more and more bodymen are taking pains to keep a car's filler content as low as possible. When the sanding dust has finally settled, a slick coat of paint is applied to complete the car's construction. *Slick*, in this case, is not just hyperbole. A properly applied paint scheme is actually good for several extra miles per hour in superspeedway velocity, over a rough primer coat of paint.

In contrast to cars of the sixties and seventies, most of whose logos and racing numbers were hand painted,

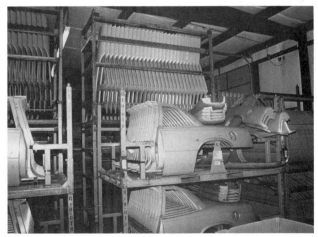

Though OEM stampings, such as these Buick quarters, serve as the basis for a Winston Cup car's sheet metal, by the time a team's fabricator is finished, precious little of their original mass is left. Usually, just bodylines are retained by car builders. The rest of a car's bodywork is then made up out of hand-formed panels of sheet metal.

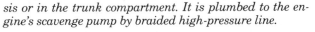

Current rules require that the reservoir to a car's dry-sump system be located either under the rear of the chassis or in the trunk compartment. It is plumbed to the engine's scavenge pump by braided high-pressure line.

Fuel cells are mandatory equipment and have been since 1967. Each 22gal bladder is mounted inside a 33x17x9in steel safety housing. The cast-aluminum fitting in the top of the tank is a safety shutoff valve that seals the tank shut in a rollover accident. Clear gas-proof tubing connects the fuel cell to both the dry-break filler neck and a body panel–mounted vent fitting.

A dry-sump oiling system is used to button up the bottom of the oil pan. As with the induction system, teams are usually secretive about the internals of their oiling system. Savvy engine builders like Robert Yates and Lou La Rosa have discovered that extra performance can be unlocked even in those areas, so hours are now spent knife-edging crank throws and close tolerance fitting oil pan baffles in an attempt to reduce parasitic losses from oil drag on the reciprocating assembly. An external scavenging system is used to route oil to and from the pan and the remote reservoir.

A set of tuned stainless steel headers round out the underhood plumbing on a race-spec Chevrolet small-block engine. Those thermally wrapped tubes then dump into a set of unmuffled collectors that snake to one side of the car or the other.

Other bits and pieces include a fixed-pitch fan (flat-blade fans are used during qualifying to satisfy the NASCAR rules book); a high-efficiency aluminum radiator; a fenderwell-mounted oil cooler; and dual coils (with one serving as a back-up), usually mounted through the firewall.

Unhampered by a rules-mandated restrictor plate, the best Chevrolet NASCAR engines are capable of something in excess of 650hp. Restrictor plates reduce that figure by at least 200 ponies.

Though it's hard to make performance characteriza-

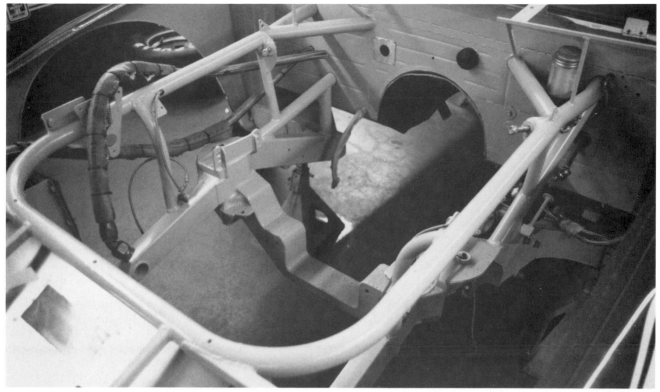

The fabricated snout and front loop found under the hood of a contemporary Winston Cup car have changed little since 1969. This is especially true in the case of rear steer cars that still use what are basically 1965 Galaxie suspension components at the bow.

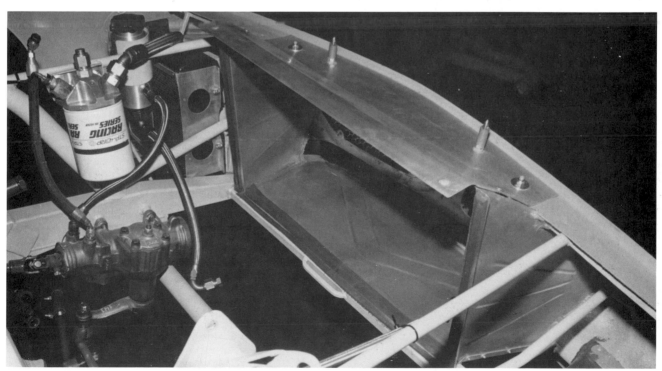

The aluminum panels and plumbing used to dress out a Winston Cup car's engine bay are often masterpieces of the fabricator's art. Air is directed to the radiator by aluminum panels that are ribbed for extra strength. The oil cooler is connected to the engine by braided steel lines, and similar high-pressure hoses are used to plumb the power steering system.

OEM tempered glass windshields are required at the front of a Winston Cup car's greenhouse. Lexan is used to fill all other window openings. The lower "wiper" lip is trimmed from each windshield before it is mounted.

When mounted, a windshield is held in place by external tabs and supported from behind by three vertical braces. Richard Petty used this brace of analog gauges to keep tabs on his engine during the 1992 season.

rpm. Hours of flow bench work go into every set of SVO heads before they are bolted on a motor. Similar to their bow-tie rivals, Ford engines are fed by a single 850cfm Holley carburetor and a high-rise aftermarket intake manifold. An equally non-Ford solid-lifter camshaft is used to control timing events, and it acts on a set of roller rockers with ratios in the 1.73:1 to 1.8:1 range.

A dry-sump oiling system is used to seal up the bottom of the block, and it nestles between a set of "full-breakdown" stainless steel headers tuned for performance in a specific rpm range. "Advertised" horsepower production from a top-performing SVO 358 is in the 625 to 650 range, but it's been widely rumored that Robert Yates has been able to coax another 50 ponies on top of that from the SVO small-blocks he builds. Whatever the figure, most of that power is found in the upper end of the rpm range. Ford motors perform best on long tracks where revs can be kept high—and that is no doubt why Bill Elliott was so awesome at Talladega and Daytona in pre-restrictor plate days. However, the high-rpm advantage formerly enjoyed by Elliott and other Ford drivers is negated by the use of those flow-restricting plates. In fact, most Ford teams complain that the plates actually hurt the performance of their engines more than they hinder the Chevrolet competition.

Jacking points like these are placed at a car's exact, race-weight center of gravity. As a result, a single jack can raise the entire side of a car during one of NASCAR's trademark pit stops.

Without a doubt, one of the most exciting aspects of the typical NASCAR race is a team's ability to change four tires, add 22gal of gas, clean the windshield, scrub the grille, and give the driver a drink—all in less than 25 seconds! The design and construction of the typical NASCAR car makes all that haste possible.

Transmissions

As different as Ford and Chevrolet engines are in mechanical design, they both usually work in tandem with identical four-speed transmissions. The two most commonly used gearboxes on the circuit are both evolutions of OEM equipment. Most popular is the aluminum-cased Borg-Warner Super T-10, which has been in use since the sixties. Though a T-10 is light in weight and rugged in construction, its biggest advantage is the wide selection of gear sets made for it by the aftermarket. That permits engine builders to tailor the performance of their race cars to the specific needs of a particular track—or even corner.

Another popular transmission on the circuit is the Jericho. Based on the Ford top loader four-speed that was a favorite of many drivers during the sixties, the Jericho has been modified to permit clutchless shifts. A wide variety of ratios are also being made for use within its aluminum case.

Modern Winston Cup cars are typically built "light"—that is to say, to top the scales at less than the 3,500lb minimum they have been required to weigh since 1987. The extra weight necessary to meet the weight rule is then strategically added to the rocker panels in the form of lead bars. In this way, weight bias, front to rear, can be precisely dialed in to suit the needs of a particular track.

A routine part of the pre-race inspection process is a trip across the official scales. Current Winston Cup rules spec-ify a minimum race weight of 3,500lb. Sixteen hundred pounds of the mass must ride on the right-side tires.

Considering the power they must deliver under incredibly demanding conditions, only the finest components make it into a NASCAR engine. Using meticulously prepared parts, crews assemble the engines with an eye for detail and precision that home mechanics can hardly imagine.

In contrast to NASCAR's OEM requirement for block and head castings, the rules allow most other parts of a stock car's powerplant can to be aftermarket in origin. Rods are typically forged steel, for example, and supplied by a specialty manufacturer.

The corporate GM engines that power Winston Cup stars like Darrell Waltrip and Dale Earnhardt are evolutions of the venerable Chevrolet small-block that made its debut in 1955. In current racing fettle, a 358ci Mouse Motor can crank out in excess of 650hp—when not hindered by an infernal restrictor plate, that is. When it is equipped with that device, power output drops more than 200 ponies.

Significant Car of the Period
Ironhead's Lumina:
A Look at the Goodwrench Chevrolet

His friends call him Ironhead, the competition calls him the Intimidator, and almost everyone else calls him one of the best seat-of-the-pants race car drivers of all time. He is, of course, Dale Earnhardt, six-time NASCAR National Champion and winner of more than fifty-two Winston Cup events. Since driving a blue-and-yellow Rod Osterland Monte Carlo to the first of those wins at Bristol in 1979, Earnhardt has come to be the one driver on the circuit most closely associated with Chevrolet. This year, as in the past, Earnhardt campaigned the Goodwrench-sponsored number 3 Chevrolet on the twenty-nine-race NASCAR circuit. Low-slung and dressed in bad-boy black racing livery, Earnhardt's 1992 Lumina looked intimidating even when at rest. It must have seemed doubly so to Brand X competitors who first saw the car loom large in their rearview mirror and then watched helplessly as it rocketed past them on the track. Because their glimpses were so fleeting and because few fans got to visit a Winston Cup garage area, we thought we'd take the chance to give Earnhardt's hapless competitors and you an "up close and personal" look at the most feared car in stock car racing.

Like all cars on the circuit, the Luminas that team owner Richard Childress prepares for Earnhardt to drive have only the most tenuous relationship with the Chevrolets on sale at your local dealership. Each of the superspeedway, intermediate-track, short-track, and road course cars in the North Carolina-based team's inventory began life as a collection of seamless square and round tube stock on a race fabricator's surface plate. Square and rectangular stock is used to form a perimeter frame that is, in turn, reinforced with a jungle gym's worth of round roll cage tubing. Suspension mounts are added next. At the rear, they accept a NASCAR-standard Ford-derived differential and the trailing arms that are used to locate it. Stiff, screw jack-adjustable coil springs provide suspension travel, and a panhard rod keeps everything centered under the chassis. Beefy floater hubs are used to prevent disaster in the case of axle breakage, and they mount massive, manhole-sized ventilated disc brakes that are acted upon by alloy calipers. A pair of gas-charged shocks and the differential cooler's plumbing complete the rear suspension.

Fabricated A-frames and special heavy-duty spindles are used at the bow, and another pair of adjustable coils is mounted between them. Two more gas shocks; a thick, through-the-frame sway bar; and another pair of locomotive-sized discs are also part of the program. The steering gear in the number 3 car is based on a power-assisted Delco-style box that acts on tie rods located ahead of the spindles. Referred to as a front steer setup, these components offer better feel and quicker rebuild time than the old "rear steer" components (tie rods and drag link behind the spindles) that used to be standard just one or two seasons ago. Stamped-steel 15x9in Bassett rims and sticky 28x10in Goodyear slicks make the completed 110in wheelbase chassis a roller.

Dale Earnhardt's sleek 1992 Lumina makes an impression wherever it goes—and that's usually to the front of the pack! His hard-charging, take-no-prisoners driving style coupled with the Lumina's sleek aerodynamics and solid mechanical package have made both hard-to-beat.

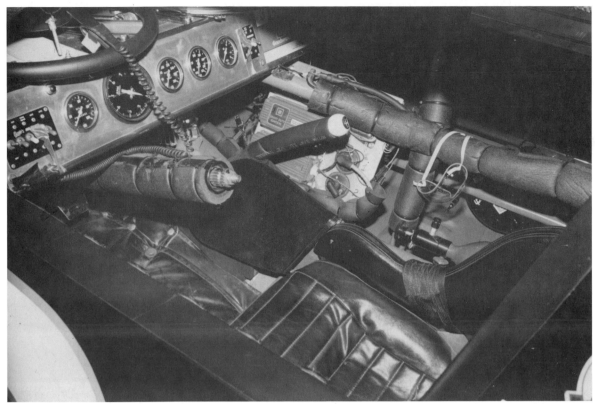

"The Intimidator," Dale Earnhardt, plots his course through traffic from within this crowded complex of roll cage tubes, ignition gear, analog gauges, and safety equipment. Note the quick-release steering wheel.

The sheet metal skin that clothes the bare chassis of one of Earnhardt's cars is, for the most part, hand formed from flat stock. Though his Luminas look disconcertingly stock to most fans in the stands, in truth, only their hood, roof panels, and deck lid ever carried a genuine GM part number. Hammer and dolly work, buckets of Bondo, and hours of expensive wind tunnel time are the basis for the rest of a Goodwrench Lumina's cosmetic configuration. A snowplowlike front air dam and a 35-degree-angled aluminum rear deck spoiler distinguish a number 3 Lumina from its grocery-getting counterparts and provide much-needed stability at racing velocities. Truth be known, the cars also vary from stock from the beltline down, too. However, strict attention is paid to maintaining the stock hood, roof, and rear deck bodyline, as official NASCAR templates permit only a 1/4in variation in this critical aerodynamic dimension.

Of course, the slickest aerodynamic package in the world would be useless without a motive force to push it through the wind. Earnhardt's Lumina receives its motorvation from a highly modified evolution of the familiar Chevrolet small-block engine first introduced in 1955. The engine size is held at 358ci by current sanctioning body rules. That displacement is reached with the help of a beefy four-bolt block that's been filled with a forged crank, trick rods, and an octet of 12.5:1 pistons. An externally scavenged dry-sump system and a track-specific flat-tappet cam dress out the short-block.

That fairly straightforward bottom end is topped off with an induction tract that has received countless hours of painstaking attention. For 1992, NASCAR specified that all the alloy small-block Chevrolet heads in the Winston Cup garage area had to incorporate either steel or titanium valves that mounted at an angle of 18 degrees relative to the centerline of the crank. Valve spacing, rocker stud location, and the external dimensions of each head casting were also specified by the rules book, as were spark plug placement and the amount of work allowed on the top of each intake port. NASCAR officials also dictate the type of intake manifold that can be used, the number and size of carburetor venturis, and the precise dimensions of the low-pressure air inlet at the base of the windshield. It is within these rules that horsepower can be found, and Earnhardt's engine builders burn tankersful of midnight oil in that pursuit. Their work currently produces more than 650hp from an unrestricted, NASCAR-legal-small-block. Bolting on the restrictor plate required at Daytona and Talladega reduces that figure by as much as 250hp—but that is still enough to propel the Goodwrench car to speeds in the neighborhood of 192mph.

Other underhood appointments include a set of equal-length headers that dump, unmuffled, into the atmosphere; a high-efficiency aluminum; and a GM-developed ignition system. High-octane Unocal racing gas is served up by high-pressure pumps, from a trunk-mounted fuel cell limited to exactly 22gal of petrol. The power produced by the fires of the internal-combustion process are handed off to an alloy-cased evolution of the Borg-Warner T-10 four-speed and finally to a track-specific set of gears. At Daytona, the number 3 car mounted those gears on a Detroit locker center section.

Winston Cup engines receive cold air from the low-pressure area at the base of the windshield. A directional scoop is permitted to channel that air to the rear of the air cleaner, but sealed systems have not been allowed since the early seventies.

With the exception of the specific type of engine in residence under the hood, the rest of a Winston Cup car's drivetrain is pretty standard—regardless of make. A three-disc clutch is used to transmit the power on tap back to a four-speed manual transmission. Two types of gearboxes are prevalent on the circuit. The most commonly used superspeedway tranny is an evolution of the Borg-Warner Super T-10. Both lightweight and rugged, the transmission also can be equipped with a variety of gear sets produced by the aftermarket. Short-track and road course cars often mount an evolution of the Ford top loader four-speed referred to as the Jericho

Right
Regardless of the marque logo they carry, NASCAR Winston Cup cars have remarkably similar body styles. That's because they're all designed to be as aerodynamic as possible within a common set of rules. If these Thunderbirds and Luminas were without their paint, some fans would hardly be able to tell them apart.

All dressed up and ready for the dance, this Ford engine carries a three-stage dry-sump system, a power steering pump, an alternator, a tuned exhaust system, and a top loader–based four-speed.

Index

Aerodynamics, 54-69, 93-105
Air jacks, 22
Air Lift air bladders, 35
Allison, Bobby, 37, 96, 98
AMA ban on racing, 14-17, 27, 42
AMA, see Automobile Manufacturers Association
AMC Matador, 39
American Motors (AMC), 32
Andretti, Mario, 53
Automobile Manufacturers Association (AMA), 14-17, 30

Baker, Buck, 13, 25-28,
Baker, Buddy, 37
Banjo's Performance Center, 107
Bettenhausen, Tony, 22
Bodine, Geoff, 101
Bodywork, 54-69, 93-105, 112-119
Brakes, 24, 38-40, 91-93, 111-112
Buick Regal, 100

Chassis, 31-38, 105-111
Chevrolet "Mystery Motor," 23-24, 31, 42-45
Chevrolet Chevelle, 55, 73-77, 112
Chevrolet engines, 119-126
Chevrolet Impala, 42-44
Chevrolet Lumina, 10, 136-140
Chevrolet Monte Carlo SS, 96, 100-101
Chevrolet Motor Division, 14-17, 23-24, 27, 31, 32, 42-45
Childress, Richard, 136-140
Chrysler Corporation, 13, 25, 30, 97
Chrysler Hemi engine, 47-48, 53-54
Curtice, Harlow H. "Red," 14, 17

Davis, Mark, 142-153
De Paolo, Pete, 13
Dieringer, Darel, 41, 50
Dodge Charger 500, 59
Dodge Charger, 55, 106-107
Dodge Daytona, 62-66
Donohue, Mark, 10, 39, 93

Earnhardt, Dale, 101, 136-140
Elliott, Bill, 100-101, 120-129
Elliott, Ernie, 127
Engines, 45-54, 119-130

Fire systems, 72
Flock, Bob, 13, 25
Flock, Fonty, 13, 25
Flock, Tim, 13, 25-26
Ford "Cammer" engine, 47-49
Ford 427 FE (High Riser) engine, 46-47
Ford 427 Tunnel Port engine, 59
Ford Boss 429 engine, 61
Ford engines, 126-130
Ford Fairlane, 53, 56
Ford Galaxie, 11, 29, 31-32, 36, 46-55, 105-111
Ford GT 40, 55

Ford GT Mark II, 55
Ford King Cobra, 66-67
Ford Motor Company, 9, 27-30, 32, 46-48
Ford Thunderbird, 10, 93-95, 99, 120-121
Ford Torino Talladega, 23, 54-69
Ford Torino, 113-114
Ford, Henry, II, 18, 29, 49
Fox, Ray, 43
Foyt, Anthony Joseph "A.J.," 18
France, William G. "Bill," Sr., 6, 13, 17-18, 20, 26-28, 46-49
Fuel cells, 72

General Motors (GM), 30, 31
Glotzbach, Charlie, 61
Golden Commando engine, 27
Goldsmith, Paul, 45

Hamilton, Pete, 67
Holbrook, Bill, 57-60
Holman & Moody (H & M), 9, 10, 21-22, 24, 28-29, 31-38, 40, 43, 51-53, 57-59
Holman, John, 13, 17, 28, 31, 43
Homologation, 13
Hudson Hornet, 9, 10, 12, 20
Hutcherson, Dick "Hutch," 35, 87-90
Hutcherson-Pagan, 107
Hyde, Harry, 63

Iacocca, Lee, 43, 67
Interiors, 112-119
Isaac, Bobby, 45, 61-66, 113-114

Johncock, Gordon, 22
Johnson, Junior, 31, 36-37, 42-44, 55-56, 96, 112

Kiekhaefer, Carl, 13, 25-26, 40
Knudsen, Semon "Bunkie," 18, 27, 60, 67

Lorenzen, Fred "Fast Freddy," 29, 36, 42-43, 51-53, 55

MacKay, Joe, 13
Matthews, Banjo, 36
McNamara, Robert S., 17, 27-28
Mercury Cyclone Spoiler II, 54-69, 102-103
Mercury Marine, 13, 25-26
Moody, Ralph, 10, 13, 17, 28, 31, 57-60, 82-86
Moore, Bud, 22, 50, 113-114, 127
Moore, Don, 45
Mundy, Frank "Rebel," 13

NASCAR (National Association for Stock Car Auto Racing), 6
NASCAR rules book, 15
NASCAR time line, 7-9
Nichels, Ray, 17

Oldsmobile Cutlass, 95
Owens, Cotton, 28

Panch, Marvin, 18, 32
Pardue, Jimmy, 41
Parsons, Benny, 95
Passino, Jacques, 57-61
Pearson, David "Silver Fox," 59, 61, 102-103
Penske, Roger, 10, 39, 93
Petty Enterprises, 33-34, 67
Petty, Lee, 12, 17, 28
Petty, Richard, 28, 33-34, 37, 40, 45, 53, 55, 61, 97, 106-107
Plymouth Belvedere, 55
Plymouth Road Runner, 67
Plymouth Satellite, 53
Pontiac Grand Prix, 101
Pontiac Motor Division, 31
Professional Driver's Association (PDA), 61

Restrictor plates, 70-71
Roberts, Glenn "Fireball," 13, 18, 22, 24, 28, 31, 35
Rodger, Robert M., 61
Roll cages, 24, 71
Rose, Mauri, 21
Rutherford, Johnny, 18, 31, 43

Safety equipment, 71-79
Screw jacks, 35, 37
Seats, 78
Shinoda, Larry, 54
Stacey, Nelson, 29
Starlift roof package, 29
Strictly Stock Division, 6
Strobe lights, 41
Sullivan, Jack, 35
Suspensions, 31-38, 105-111

Thomas, Herb, 13, 18
Thompson, Speedy, 13, 25-26, 28
Tire inner liner, 41
Tires, 40-45, 80-81, 111-112
Torrence, Wayne, 80-81
Transmissions, 130
Turner, Curtis, "Pops," 13, 55

Unser, Bobby, 18

Wade, Billy, 41
Waltrip, Darrell, 100
Weatherly, Joe "Little Joe," 13
Wheels, 40-45, 111-112
White, Rex, 31
Wood Brothers, 28, 59, 102-103
Wood, Glenn, 102-103
Wood, Leonard, 102-103

Yarborough, Cale, 59, 67
Yarbrough, LeeRoy, 59, 61
Yates, Robert, 127-129, 154-159
"Yellow Banana," 50, 55, 112
Yunick, Henry "Smokey," 13, 18-24, 31-32, 35, 37, 40, 43, 55, 73-77